Karen Durski

D0908587

Finding Grandma's European Ancestors

By Stephen Szabados

Dedication

To my wife Susan
and
My fantastic grandsons whose smiles
inspire my genealogy research

Cover Photo: My great-grandmother and her three children that immigrated with her from Pankota, Hungary. My grandfather is standing at the left of the picture. Circa 1910

Copyright © 2012 **Stephen M Szabados**

All rights reserved.

ISBN: 1468128450

ISBN-13: 978-1468128451

CONTENTS

ACKNOWLEDGMENTS

I would like to thank the many people that have been very patient and very tolerant with my many questions. These include many fellow researchers and also friends and relatives who had to put-up with my many stories. Anthony Kierna at the Schaumburg Township District Library and Michael Mulholland at the Arlington Height Memorial Library were especially helpful with their review and comments of the contents of this book.

Introduction

My initial genealogical research was to satisfy my curiosity about my family history but now my priority is to pass along a well documented and rich history for my children and grandchildren. I have also expanded my research beyond my immediate ancestors to include the ancestors of my son-in-law and daughter-in-law so my grandchildren will have a complete picture of their family history.

I began my research on the Internet using a free trial offer from Ancestry.com. After I found my first census record, I became addicted to seeing a part of me in the documents and pictures of my ancestors. I spent many days working eight hours at the office and then eight to ten hours at home researching genealogy online. Using the internet allowed me to find many documents very quickly without leaving home. After exhausting most of the online databases, my research expanded to libraries, local archives and county records.

The purpose of this book is to describe the steps that I followed to find the birthplaces of my ancestors and their documents to help other researchers in their work.

Note that my research has been in the records found in Poland, Hungary, Romania, Slovenia (was part of Austria and then Yugoslavia), Bohemia (now Czech Republic), Russia and Germany. The steps that I used to find my ancestors can also be used to research immigrants from other countries of Europe.

My Story

About 55 years ago when I was in grade school, I asked my grandmother Anna Chmielewski where she was born and the names of her parents because I was interested in knowing my family history. She told me their names and where she was born and I wrote them down. However, I lost my notes from this conversation and I did not return to my genealogy research until after my grandmother and mother had died.

With my mother and grandmother dead, the only source of information to find where to find my Polish ancestors was in the U.S. documents. I found documents that indicated that my grandmother left Poland in 1921 and immigrated to Camden, New Jersey to live with her brother Hipolit. She married my grandfather Steve John Zuchowski in 1923 and moved to Bloomington, Illinois. Using various documents for my grandmother and her brother, I found a number of town names that were clues to locating her birthplace.

- Andrzejewo – was on her marriage certificate & Naturalization petition
- Przezdziecko & Ostrow – was on her passenger manifest
- Pierzchaly & Lomza – was on her brother's passenger manifest

Please note that you should search for all documents that list your ancestor and also their siblings and other relatives to find as many town names as possible. Since they were all born in the same town or area, the information for siblings and relatives will lead you to the same birthplace as your ancestor.

After more research using gazetteers and maps, I found the locations of eight towns with the name Andrzejewo but only one that was near Ostrow and Lomza. When I found this one town on a map I saw that it was near a small village with the name Przezdziecko-Pierzhaly. This led me to finding the birthplace of my grandmother and her ancestors. Documents that I found indicated:

1. Anna and her brother were born in the village of <u>Przezdziecko-Pierzhaly</u> which is in the voivodeship (province) of <u>Lomza</u> and in the Powiat (county or district) of <u>Ostrow</u>
2. She was baptized in the town of <u>Andrzejewo</u> which was where the parish church was located

Note that the village of Przezdziecko-Pierzhaly has a two part name and I found the two parts on different documents.

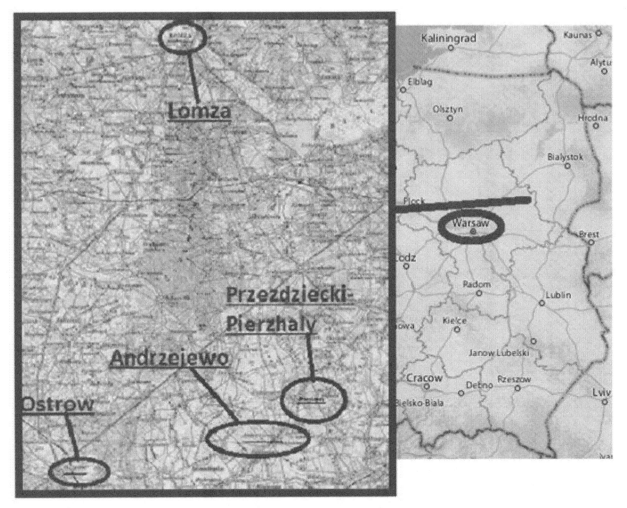

Location of town names found

The above illustration of finding Anna Chmielewski's ancestors is a very good example of the steps needed to find your ancestors in the "old country". The following pages will discuss these steps in detail.

Where do you start?

To begin your journey to your ancestral home, you will need to identify where you are going. To find this place on a map, you need to identify as many place names as possible on the documents that you find for your ancestors and their siblings and relatives. If their passenger manifest listed their destination was to a friend, include this friend in your research since they also came from the same place. Treat these place names as clues because they are usually not spelled correctly and there are many town names that have multiple locations. Look for your clues in various documents and in the stories told by your older relatives. If your immigrant ancestors did not save copies of the documents that they received when they left the "Old Country" you will need to find the U.S. documents that list clues.

You need to Identify:
- the general area that they left.
- the name of the village or town.
- the name of the town where the church or civil records were recorded.
- as many town names as possible to confirm where to look.

Envision a map of the area around the birthplace of your ancestor and each clue that you find is a piece of the jigsaw puzzle that has a picture of this map on it. Once you fit all of clues together, the picture on the jigsaw puzzle comes together and you will be able to recognize where the area is located.

Four steps to find the birthplace of your ancestors:

1. Find town names for clues
2. Learn the history of the country and the possible areas
3. Use Gazetteers and maps to determine how clues fit together
4. Find records and translate them

Step One – Find town names associated to your ancestor from many sources.

The search that we are about to start is for your ancestors who immigrated. We need to find where they were born in the "old country." Below is a list of documents where you can find a town name that will be a clue to finding the birthplace of your immigrant ancestor. Do not stop the search when you find one name. Collect as many names as possible. Most countries have multiple locations for towns with the same name so you will need to have more than one place name to point the way. Also you research the documents of brothers, sisters, aunts, uncles and friends of your ancestors if they were born in the "old country". The place names on documents for these relatives should be in the same locale as your ancestors. After you have exhausted your search through the documents, you will find that one of the names may be the name of the province, another one the county, another the town where the parish church is located and others may be surrounding villages. You will be able to locate your ancestor's birthplace by finding an area on a map that has all of the names that you found.

Most of the sources listed below are documents that were generated in the United States. Do not neglect to search the "old shoe boxes" or desk drawers that may contain letters and documents from the "old country." Also interview your older relatives.

Here is a list of documents and sources that are useful in finding town name clues:
- Documents and letters from old country (such as Birth documents)
- Family oral history – interview older relatives
- Marriage records – civil and church records
- Naturalization petitions - 1906 and after
- Passenger manifests
- Social Security Applications
- Military Records
- Employment records
- Death certificates
- Obituaries

Now let's discuss each document and source in detail.

- ### *Documents from old country*
Search the desk drawers, file cabinets and shoe boxes for "old papers" to see if your immigrant ancestors saved documents from the "old country". If you are lucky and find their baptismal certificate or exit visa (passport), you will have very accurate information and probably have all that you need to find their birthplace on a map. Old letters and post cards from the "old country" are also very valuable. The letters may be from friends or relatives that still lived in the area of your ancestor's birth or may contained references to where your ancestor left.

Below is a copy of the baptismal certificate for my grandfather Steve John Zuchowski. Note that on the certificate his name appears in Polish as Szezepan Jan Zochowski. Be prepared to accept alternate spellings of names and places as you do your research.

I found the certificate in my mother's papers after her death. Most documents like this are carried by the immigrants when they leave their home but note that my grandfather's document is dated 1959 (he immigrated to America in 1912). He probably requested this copy of his baptismal certificate as proof of birth when he applied for Medicare benefits. Three of the sections that I highlighted with a rectangle list the town of Czyzewo and the fourth rectangle lists the village of Dmochich-Kudly. There are a number of towns in Poland named with variations of Czyzew but only one that have neighboring villages that have names starting with Dmochy. The translation reveals that the village where he was born was Dmochy Kudly and the parish church where he was baptized was in Czyzew. **(*Czyzew is the key piece of information since this would be the location of the parish church which is the source for records for his parents and ancestors.*)**

The document also lists the names of his parents. Unfortunately the form that was used to make a copy of the information from the original church register did not have a space for the names of the grandparents. I have found many registers from this time period sometimes listed the names of the grandparents also. Knowing these names on the birth record would help me find the birth records of Steve's parents faster and with more accuracy.

Baptismal Certificate for Steve Zuchowski

Below are two examples of records that were carried from the "old country." They are the birth record and the exit visa for Wenzel (James) Syrovatka that were found in a desk drawer of my wife's great-aunt after she died. Note that the birth record listed his parents and also his grandparents. Both documents listed his birthplace as Gross (Large) Doubrava and the exit visa also listed that he was born in the Bezirke (district) of Moldaistein and the Kreis (State) of Budweis. The upper left hand corner of the birth certificate also lists more place names. The Diocese is listed as Budejovice (Budweis) with the Parsonage at Bechyně and the rectory at Chrášťany.

These documents point to the exact location of Wensel's birth because there were a number of villages named Doubrava but only one in the state of Budweis and near Chrášťany. The added bonus from these documents was the names of the grandparents plus the rich visual history the appearance of these old documents gives to the family history. Finding these documents led to more records that traced the family's roots back to about 1730. Pictures and an article about the area's history were also found on the county website for Chrášťany and these added more rich history to the family's heritage.

Birth Certificate for Wenzel Syrovatka carried by him from Bohemia

In the late 1800s, men had to obtain permission to leave their villages and emigrate. When requesting a passport, they had to submit several documents including a copy of the birth record, marriage, evidence of residence and occupation, supporting documents, and references. Applicants had to sign that they would waive their residence right to live in the village. If not, the village could be held liable for paying for return costs if emigration was refused or the people came back for other reasons.

The age and status of the man was one reason why emigration could be refused. Men had to prove that their military service obligation had been completed before they could leave. Sometimes this meant serving the required years or paying for someone else to take their place.

Also note that these legal documents were required by the passenger lines before passage could be sold to the immigrant. These legal documents would make it impossible for the name of the immigrant to be changed by the passenger line clerk or the immigration clerk in America.

1876 Exit Visa for Wenzel (James) Sirovatka

To find personal documents such as baptismal certificates, passports, letters and postcards from the "old country", search the papers of your parents and grandparents. If any were saved they will be treasures because they usually list the birthplaces of the immigrant ancestors. These treasures may not be in the papers saved by your mother or grandmother but could be with other relatives. Your immigrant ancestors may have lived with one of their children before they died. If they remained in the home until they died, one or two of the children may have watched over them. Track the descendants of these caretakers who may have sorted through all of the papers and pictures in the home and saved some of them. If you find documents with other relatives, ask for copies of the documents and offer to share the results of your research. Also be very careful with the originals since they may be very fragile due to age. Use copies or electronic scans in your research and store the originals in a safe place.

Summary for personal papers

1. Search desk drawers, file cabinets and shoe boxes for birth records, baptismal certificates, exit visas and pictures.
2. Track down descendants of caretakers of ancestors before they died.
3. Exchange and share information and documents with other relatives

• *Talk to older relatives*

Next, begin showing your research to your older relatives and interviewing them in order to see if they have any oral history or documents to add to your research.

Saving oral history is a critical early step in your genealogical research. A great deal of family history is passed down orally through the generations. Your family's oral history may involve stories of the immigration of the family to America or it may be as simple as saving a family recipe. Remember that you are seeking information from older members of the family and their memories are at risk of being lost to time. Therefore, it should be a priority to interview your patriarchs and matriarchs of the family. They could be your grandparents, great-grandparents, granduncles, grandaunts, great-granduncles, great-grandaunts and older cousins. Even older neighbors and acquaintances of these people may have information to add. Identify the individuals in your family that seem to know the most family history and interview them as early in your research as possible.

Prepare for your visit with relatives by developing a list of questions and topics to cover. It is important to do this because it will help focus your conversation and the answers will help you fill in the blanks on the family tree. Obtaining the full names including nicknames and maiden names of all the relatives is very important at the start of your research. Familysearch.org has an article on their Wiki pages that lists over 1800 sample questions that can be used when interviewing older relatives. The list is available on line at:

https://wiki.familysearch.org/en/Creating_A_Personal_History.

Also prepare for your interviews by organizing the information that you have already found. I suggest that you send your relative a note before the interview and share with them some of the questions that you may ask them. The note may help open up the subconscious of your relatives by giving them time to remember the family stories that they heard when they were young.

Extract all of the information from documents and start to compile summaries for each ancestor. Organize your documents in ring binders or folders. Include pictures of your ancestors in their sections. Show your relatives these summaries and pictures. The summaries and pictures will help establish rapport with family members and put your relatives at ease. Reviewing your research will help them recall the oral history that they have stored in their sub-conscious.

The interviews should be an equal exchange of information. The questions should flow as normal conversation and not as an interrogation. Avoid questions that seek a "Yes" or "No" answer. This gives your relatives a chance to tell their stories. Try to be a good listener:

• Don't talk or interrupt while the person is speaking.

- Don't put words in their mouths.
- Don't finish their sentences for them either.
- Let them speak until they have completed their thought before you go on to the next question.
- Include pictures in your research and ask your relatives to help identify the people in the pictures.

Try to either videotape or audio record these conversations so that you have an accurate record of their comments. If using a video camera, try to have a second person control it and use a tripod to steady the filming. Taping the interview will free you up to interact with your relative and your eye contact with them may make them more comfortable so they may remember more oral history.

Don't try to complete the Interview in one sitting. You should keep your interviews to no more than a couple of hours unless the person feels otherwise. People get tired after talking for a while. You should plan on more than one session. This gives you a chance to follow-up on various aspects of the oral history that you capture and also gives your relative time to remember more aspects of the family history.

The interview may also reveal that other members of the family are doing genealogy research and this could lead to exchanging more information and copies of documents.

Also remember that memories often fade and facts get confused with other facts. However, the information you obtain through oral interviews may exist nowhere else and must be taken at face value. Of particular value is information associated with pictures, documents, and other records. Also of interest are the stories, anecdotes and family traditions. Treat the oral history that you hear as treasures. However, if some of the facts do not seem accurate, remember that some parts are probably true so include all of the stories and add your comments and concerns. Future generations may be able to find more facts that sort out your concerns and resolve the problem areas of the stories.

After the interview, transcribe your conversations if you used recording equipment. If you did not record the conversation, review and summarize your notes while the conversation is still fresh in your mind. Make lists of future questions and lists of future research that are needed.

Summary of interviewing

1. Interviewing older relatives is a critical early phase of genealogical research
2. Interview relatives as soon as possible
3. Interviews should be an equal exchange of information and should not be interrogation.
4. Establish rapport with family members prior to interviewing them
5. Avoid questions that seek a "Yes" or "No" answer
6. Record interviews if possible
7. Try to check information from Oral History – treat information as clues
8. Re-visit your relative after you have new and interesting information to show them. This may turn on the memory for another story for them to tell you.

- ## *Marriage Records*

Marriage records may also be a great source to find the birthplace of your ancestor. Remember that you are searching for the marriage record for your immigrant ancestors and his siblings and cousins who were born in the "old country." Churches and governments often kept marriage records before they began documenting births and deaths. Also remember that if the ceremony was performed in a church, the event would have been recorded in both the civil registers and the church registers. Most marriage applications ask where the bride and groom were born and most church registers have a space in the record for where they were baptized. Always look in both places for the marriage record because one record may list more information about the town such as district or county. Since the bride and groom are there to give the information, the information should be accurate although spelling errors may occur.

The first step to find the marriage record for your ancestor will be finding out when they were married. Use the following sources for finding when your ancestors were married:

1. If a family bible exists look there first.
2. Family oral history may give an approximate time but this may be a very vague and inaccurate date.
3. Another important source to find the date is the 1900, 1910 and 1930 Federal census records which list information that you can use to calculate the approximate year of the marriage. The 1900 and 1910 census records list the number of years they were married and the 1930 record lists the age when they were first married. After doing the math you will have the approximate year of the marriage. Although, this is not an exact date it will help narrow the search. Note that the 1930 census asked for their age at the time of their first marriage and if you find that the number of years married for the spouses do not match, the spouse with the greater number of years was probably married to a prior wife.

Find out when your ancestor married - 1900, 1910 & 1930 Census will give approximate year

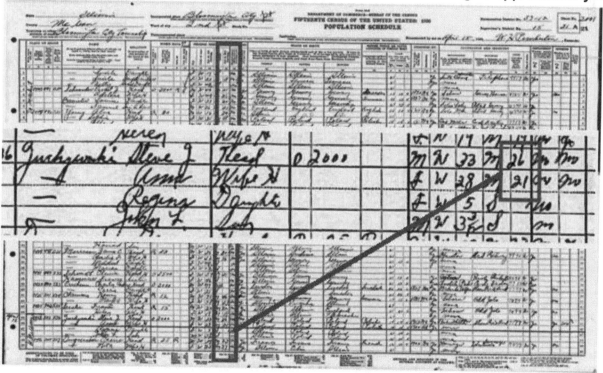

4. Online marriage indexes by state usually cover a limited time range but if your ancestor is listed you will then have both the "when" and the "where" information you need to get the actual document. The Family Search Wiki page titled "Summary of United States Marriage Records' lists the available online marriage indexes by state that are in the databases at familysearch.org and ancestry.com. I have found some indexes by googling the phrase "XXXXX marriage index'" where XXXX is the name of the state of interest. Using this method I have found marriage indexes for Illinois, for Wisconsin, for Minnesota and the Western States (this index includes Alaska, Arizona, California, Colorado, Idaho, Montana, Nevada, New Mexico, Oregon, Utah, Washington and Wyoming).

Sample of State of Illinois Marriage Index at
http://www.cyberdriveillinois.com/departments/archives/marriage.html

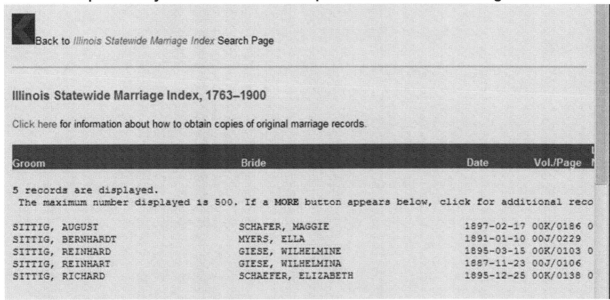

5. Other important sources for marriage information are the files of the local genealogical and historical societies. Many of these groups have copied pages or extracted information from local newspapers on marriages and deaths. Their websites usually list their collections and most will provide copies of the information for a nominal fee. Find their website, check their collections and then call or write them with your request. . Search the genealogy websites by state, county and ethnic group to find these marriage indexes.

Below is a portion of the directory for the Polish Genealogical Society of America (located in Chicago) and it shows the lists of marriage indexes for the Polish churches in Chicago and nearby counties (see below). I have also found marriage information on many county genealogy websites.

PGSA Marriage Indexes

- Marriage Records - In addition to the following, look in this directory for a specific city or region.
  - **Marriage Indices for Parishes in Poland**
  - **Marriage Index to Polish Parishes in Chicago thru 1915**
  - **Genealogical Hints**
  - **Poznan Marriage Project**
    An index of marriages from the former Polish province of Poznan (Posen).
  - St. Joseph County, IN
    - **Marriage Record Database**
  - St. Paul, MN and vicinity
    - **Birth/Baptism Record Database**
    - **Marriage Record Database**

Determine where they were married
Before you request marriage records you will have to know where they were married. Of course if the marriage is found in one of the indexes, the location should also be indicated. If census records were the

only indicator of when they were married, then the county listed on the census record may be where they were married if they did not move after the marriage. However, sometimes they may have been married in nearby counties instead of the county listed on the census. This change in the county may have been due to the location of the church or that they chose to be married in a county that had easier marriage restrictions or they may have been married at a romantic location.

Where to obtain marriage records

I have found online marriage records for the state of Washington and for Cook County Illinois. However, for other locations the marriage records normally are obtained from county offices or state archives. If you have identified the church where they were married, calling the church may find a helpful secretary who could send you a copy of the record. However, you may have to review the church records in person to obtain your information. Another important source for civil and church marriage records is the films from Family Search Centers. The films cover a limited time range but if the year of the marriage is not available on the films, then county and state records would be your only source.

Also remember to search for marriage records for children, siblings and other relatives who were born in the "old country" and married in America.

Below is the marriage application for my grandparents that I obtained from the McLean County Clerk's office in Bloomington Illinois. The clerk's office charged $15 for the two page copy which included the application and the certificate. Note that the name of her birthplace is misspelled but it did give me a name for a clue. Note that it also gave the names of her parents which were also a major help in tracing my grandmother's ancestors.

Marriage license application for Anna Chmielewski

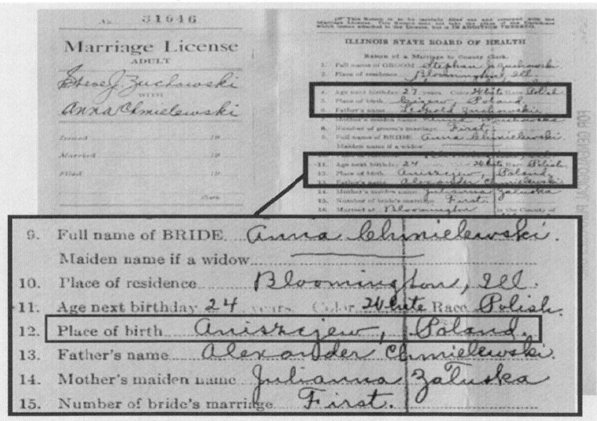

I have found that some counties saved only a copy of the marriage license and not the application. The license usually does not indicate where the bride and groom were born. In this case, check the license for the name of who performed the marriage. If the marriage was performed by a minister or priest, you will have a clue on where to look for the church record. Another indicator to find the church record is the religion and ethnic background of your ancestor. Small areas may have had only one church of a specific religion. Also in large urban areas, certain churches attracted one ethnic group because the service was performed in their native language.

Below is a copy of the page from the marriage register of St Ludmila's Church in Chicago that lists the marriage of Mary Strugar who was the sister of my wife's grandmother. St Ludmilla's was attended by the Slovenian immigrants who had immigrated to Chicago. Note that this register has a column for the date and place of Baptism (Datum et Locus Baptismi). Catholic priests would normally list the parish of baptism in his marriage register to insure that both the bride and groom were baptized so he could perform the marriage in the church. This copy was obtained from a Family History Center (FHC) film. The FHC films were created through efforts by the Church of the Latter Day Saints to help document their ancestors. I was able to rent this film at one of the Family History Centers and found this document by viewing the film.

Church marriage register for Mary Strugar (sister of my wife's grandmother)

Summary for marriage records
1. Find out when ancestors were married in U.S. – family bible, census records or online indexes
2. Find out where couple was married – family bible, census records or online indexes
3. Where to obtain documents – county clerks, state archives, Church registers, FHC films, online databases

- ## *Naturalization Petitions*

Over the years, naturalization laws changed numerous times, but generally speaking the process required a Declaration of Intention and a Petition to be filed to become a citizen. Naturalization forms prior to 1906 included country of original, date of naturalization and the court where they were naturalized and did not include where they born or any other genealogical information. After 1906, the certificate of arrival was created during the naturalization process. The immigrant also had to be a resident in the United States 5 years and a 1 year resident in the state before becoming a citizen. The naturalization process was completed in a court of law. This could be done in any local or Federal court. The court where the naturalization took place may be one place to look for the various naturalization documents.

Naturalization petitions submitted after 1906 will have a birthplace listed. The name listed could be the actual birthplace but may also be where your ancestor was baptized. Either name will be an accurate name to direct you to where to look for the records of your ancestor in the "old country". Note that there may still be variations in how the name is written if the immigrant was not literate and the person filling out the form wrote the name phonetically. You will still need to find more names that will indicate what area the birthplace is located but you will have a very accurate piece to your puzzle.

Below is the naturalization petition for my grandmother. It lists her birthplace as Andrejowo, Poland. There are a number of towns in Poland with this name so this entry only serves as one clue and other names are needed to find the exact location.

Naturalization Petitions after 1906

Petitions submitted prior to 1906 did not require a town name. The pre-1906 petition usually listed only the country of birth.

Pre 1906 Naturalization Index card

Pre-1906 Naturalization Petition

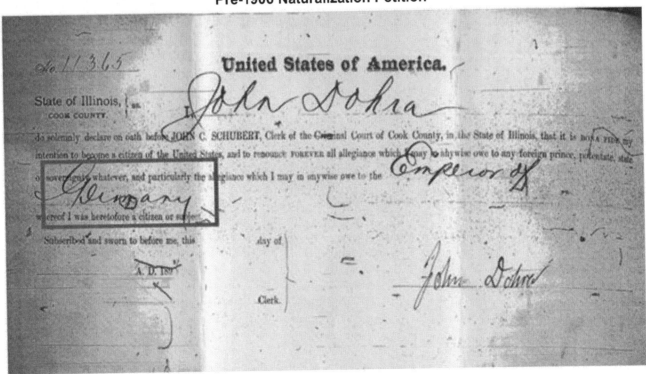

Where to obtain Naturalization petitions

Before requesting a copy of the naturalization petition, you should try to confirm that your ancestor was naturalized. The federal census records for 1900, 1910, 1920, 1930 and 1940 have a column that asks status of citizenship. Start by reviewing the 1940 census and then work back through the years until the census record indicates that your ancestor was not naturalized. This will give an estimate that they were naturalized between the two census years. If your ancestor did not become a citizen, search for naturalization papers for children and other relatives who were born in the "old country".

Other sources that may indicate if your ancestor became a citizen are naturalization indexes on ancestry.com and various county websites.

Below is a copy of the Naturalization Index card for that I downloaded from Ancestry.com for my grandmother. Note that it lists that she was naturalized in the Circuit Court of McLean County in Bloomington, Illinois.

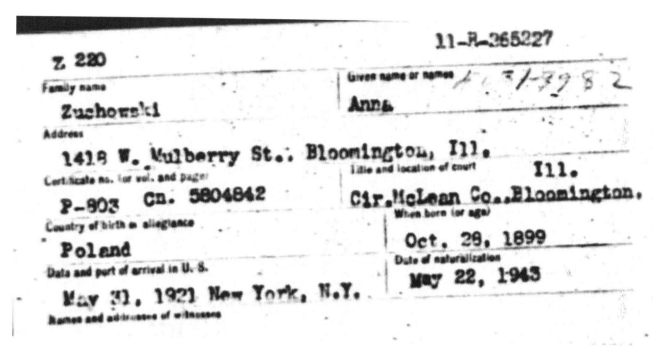

I also found my grandmother's naturalization information listed on the McLean County, Illinois website. Below is the information for my grandmother that is listed on Mclean County's Immigration page. Note that it is an extraction of information from her naturalization petition that is on file in the court records. Volunteers from the McLean County Genealogy Society extracted the information from these court files and compiled the database that is available on the McLean County website.

120 ZUCHOWSKI, ANNA Pet. for Nat. 803
Res. 1418 W. Mulberry St., Bloomington, Ill.; Housewife; b. 28 Oct. 1899 Andrejowo, Poland; Husband Steve John Zuchowski; mar. 14 July 1923 Bloomington, Ill.; he b. Poland 24 Dec. 1897; 2 children: John b. 18 Jan. 1927 Bloomington; Regina b. 19 May 1924 Bloomington; To US from Liverpool, Eng. to NY under name of Anna Chmielewski 31 May 1921 vessel unknown; Witnesses: Paul F. Jabsen, Heating Contractor; Martha Zulz, housewife; Oath of Allegiance 22 May 1943; Cert. Nat. 5804842

The next illustration is the home page for the Mclean County offices. Note the box where I point out where to select the immigration information page on the McLean County website.

Although the McLean County index gave me most of the pertinent information from my grandmother's naturalization petition, you should always obtain a copy of the actual document. Sometimes errors are made when extracting the information and the letters of written information may be interpreted incorrectly and names are misspelled.

I have also found extracted naturalization information at the website for the Clerk of the Circuit Court of Cook County.

The Stark County Ohio website goes further and offers you the ability to download the actual documents. The next illustration is the naturalization petition for my great-grandmother Elizabeth Kovacs that I downloaded from their website. Note that I have highlighted her birthplace as Kigjos, Bekes, Hungary and this was all the information that I needed to find her birth record.

ORIGINAL
(To be retained by
Clerk of Court)

UNITED STATES OF AMERICA

Vol. 79 P-251
No. 17651

PETITION FOR NATURALIZATION

[Of a Married Person, under Sec. 310(a) or (b), ~~or 315~~ of the Nationality Act of 1940 (54 Stat. 1144-1145)]

To the Honorable the ....COMMON PLEAS.............. Court of .SUMMIT COUNTY........ at ....AKRON, OHIO......
This petition for naturalization, hereby made and filed pursuant to Section 310(a) or (b), or Section 311 or 312, of the Nationality Act of 1940, respectfully shows:

(1) My full, true, and correct name is ..ELIZABETH KOVACS.........

(2) My present place of residence is ..208 E. Voris St., Akron, Summit, Ohio. (3) My occupation is ......housewife......

(4) I am ....62..... years old. (5) I was born on ....Oct. 29, 1878.......... Kisjos, Bekes, Hungary

(6) My personal description is as follows: Sex ..female.. color ..white.. complexion ..med.. color of eyes ..blue.. color of hair ..br... height ..4.. feet ..11.. inches,
weight ..164.. pounds; visible distinctive marks ....none........ race ..Magyar.. present nationality ..Hungary..

(7) I am ..now.. married; the name of my husband is ..Joseph.............. we were married on ..June 29, 1929....

at ..Akron, Ohio........; he was born at ..Szakaly, Hungary........ on ..Mar. 17, 1881....

entered the United States at ..New York, NY........ on ..Sept. 29, 1912.. permanent residence in the United States, and now resides at

..with me............ and was naturalized on ..Mar. 27, 1927.. at ..Akron, Ohio....

certificate No. ..2150791........ or became a citizen by
(7a) (If petition is filed under Section 311, Nationality Act of 1940) I have resided in the United States in marital union with my United States citizen spouse for at least 1 year immediately preceding the date of filing this petition for naturalization.
(7b) (If petition is filed under Section 312, Nationality Act of 1940) My husband or wife is a citizen of the United States, is in the employment of the Government of the United States, or of an American institution of research recognized as such by the Attorney General of the United States, or an American firm or corporation engaged in whole or in part in the development of foreign trade and commerce of the United States, or a subsidiary thereof; and such husband or wife is regularly stationed abroad in such employment. I intend in good faith to take up residence within the United States immediately upon the termination of such employment abroad.

(8) I have ..two.... children; and the name, sex, date and place of birth, and present place of residence of each of said children who is living, are as follows:
....(f) Elizabeth, born May 12, 1898 at Arad, Hungary, now res. Bloomington, Ill
....(m) George, " Sept. 21, 1904 " " " " Akron, Ohio

(9) My last place of foreign residence was ..Pankota, Arad, Hungary.. (10) I emigrated to the United States from ..Fiume, Italy..

..............(11) My lawful entry for permanent residence in the United States was at ..New York, NY............ under the name

of ..Takacs, Erzsebet............ on ..June 29, 1910.. on the SS Carpathia.. as shown by the certificate of my arrival attached to this petition.

(12) Since my lawful entry for permanent residence, I have ..not.. been absent from the United States, for a period or periods of 6 months or longer, as follows:

DEPARTED FROM THE UNITED STATES			RETURNED TO THE UNITED STATES		
PORT	DATE (Month, day, year)	VESSEL OR OTHER MEANS OF CONVEYANCE	PORT	DATE (Month, day, year)	VESSEL OR OTHER MEANS OF CONVEYANCE
none					

(13) (Declaration of intention not required) (14) It is my intention in good faith to become a citizen of the United States and to renounce absolutely and forever all allegiance and fidelity to any foreign prince, potentate, state, or sovereignty of whom or which at this time I am a subject or citizen, and it is my intention to reside permanently in the United States. (15) I am not, and have not been for the period of at least 10 years immediately preceding the date of this petition, an anarchist; nor a believer in the unlawful damage, injury, or destruction of property, or sabotage; nor a disbeliever in or opposed to organized government; nor a member of or affiliated with any organization or body of persons teaching disbelief in or opposition to organized government. (16) I am able to speak the English language (unless physically unable to do so). (17) I am, and have been during all of the periods required by law, attached to the principles of the Constitution of the United States and well disposed to the good order and happiness of the United States. (18) I have resided continuously in the United States of America for the term of ..3.... years at least immediately preceding the date of this petition, to wit: since ..June 29, 1910.. (19) I have ..not.. heretofore made petition for naturalization

number .... on .... at .... in the .... Court, and such petition was dismissed or denied by that Court for the following reasons and causes, to wit: ....
.... and the cause of such dismissal or denial has since been cured or removed.
(20) Attached hereto and made a part of this, my petition for naturalization, are a certificate of arrival from the Immigration and Naturalization Service of my said lawful entry into the United States for permanent residence (if such certificate of arrival be required by the naturalization law), and the affidavits of at least two verifying witnesses required by law.
(21) Wherefore, I, your petitioner for naturalization, pray that I may be admitted a citizen of the United States of America, and that my name be changed to ....

(22) I, aforesaid petitioner, do swear (affirm) that I know the contents of this petition for naturalization subscribed by me, that the same are true to the best of my own knowledge, except as to matters therein stated to be alleged upon information and belief, and that as to those matters I believe them to be true, and that this petition is signed by me with my full, true name: SO HELP ME GOD.

X Elizabeth Kovacs

FORM N-406
U.S. DEPARTMENT OF JUSTICE
Immigration and Naturalization Service
(Edition of 7-15-41)

416—18450

Naturalization papers generated prior to 1906 should be held by the local courts where the immigrants were naturalized. After 1906, the courts were instructed to forward all naturalization papers to federal authorities and should now be held by the National Archives. However I have found some post 1906 naturalization papers that were still being held by county authorities. I would recommend requesting naturalization papers for your ancestors first from the National archives and if they can not supply you with a copy, You should then request the papers from the county court clerk where your ancestor lived. Some counties have indexed these records on line where you can search to see if the records for your ancestor are available from the county.

Below is the home page for the US National Archives and you will start the process to order naturalization petitions by selecting the "Shop Online" box. On the next page you want to select the "Request and Order Reproductions" box.

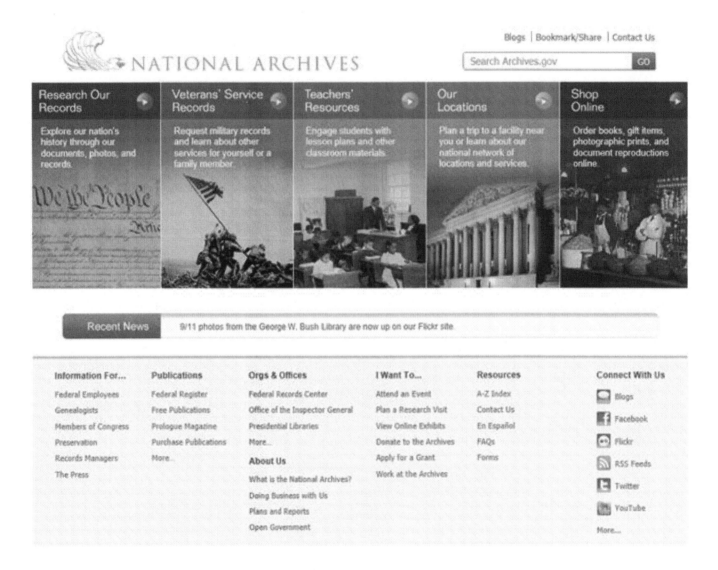

Continue going through 2-3 more pages until you are asked to fill out an online form with your ancestor's information.

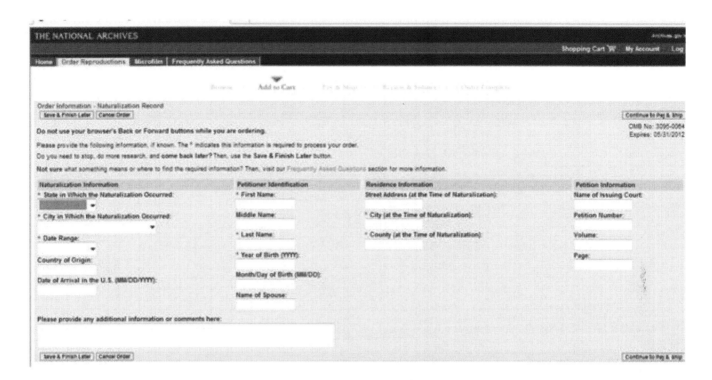

The researchers at the National Archive will respond to your request within 1-2 weeks. If they find the requested documents they will mail it to you and charge your credit card. If they do not find the documents they will give you some suggestions on where you can look next.

Summary for Naturalization Petitions
> 1. Naturalization petitions submitted after 1904 will have a birthplace listed.
> 2. Check the Clerk of the County where ancestors lived to see if they list information for Naturalization petitions or their availability.
> 3. If the County website does not offer naturalization petitions, use National Archive website to request petitions.

• *Passenger Manifests*

Passenger manifests will list one to four town names depending on the year of immigration. I have found that the town names listed have been very helpful in my research but the spelling of the names usually have problems. Most immigrants were illiterate so their information was usually entered on the document phonetically. This led to many misspellings but remembering that the names were written phonetically should still prove helpful.

The myth of name changes

Many family oral histories believe that family names were changed when immigrants entered America. However, this is a myth. Names on passenger manifests were based on official documents presented by the immigrant to the ship line at the time of boarding. It would be illegal to change their names. If families changed the spelling of their surnames they did it after arrival and usually due to daily problems in its use and to make it easier for the people around them to pronounce their name. Also, immigration stations were staffed with large numbers of translators to help insure the information that was given by the immigrants was recorded accurately.

The format of the passenger manifests that US immigration officials required changed over the years. Below is a review of when and where town names were listed on passenger manifest:

- 1908 & after: This format has two pages - birthplace is listed in the far right column on the second page, column 10 lists the last residence of the immigrant, column 11 lists a relative they left and where that relative lived
- 1906 & 1907: Birthplace is listed in the far right column, the last residence of the immigrant is listed in column 10
- Before 1906: column 10 lists the last residence of the immigrant
- Pre- 1890: column lists what country they left (occasionally an area or town was also listed)

Below are examples of each format.

Example of Passenger Manifest 1908 & after - left side of page

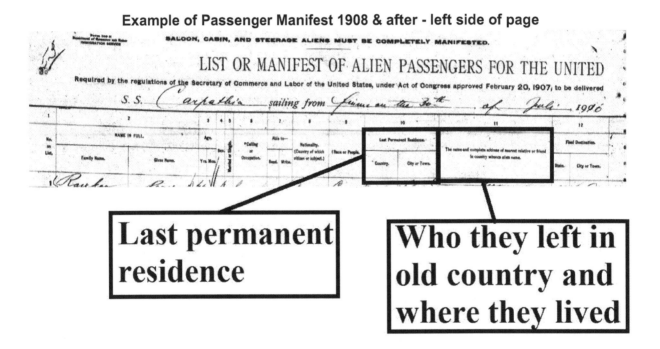

Example of Passenger Manifest 1908 & after - right side of page

Passenger Manifest for Martin Szabados
– format used 1906 & 1907

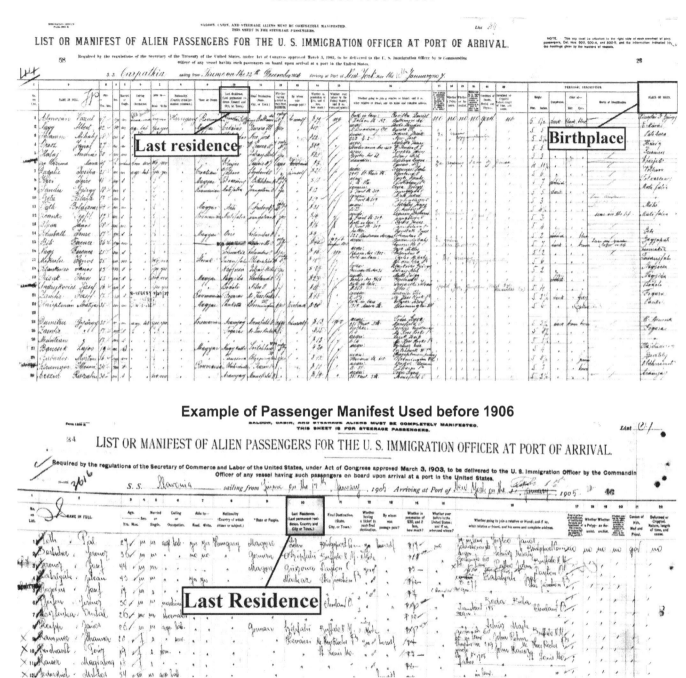

Example of Passenger Manifest Used before 1906

Example of Early Passenger Manifest – pre-1890

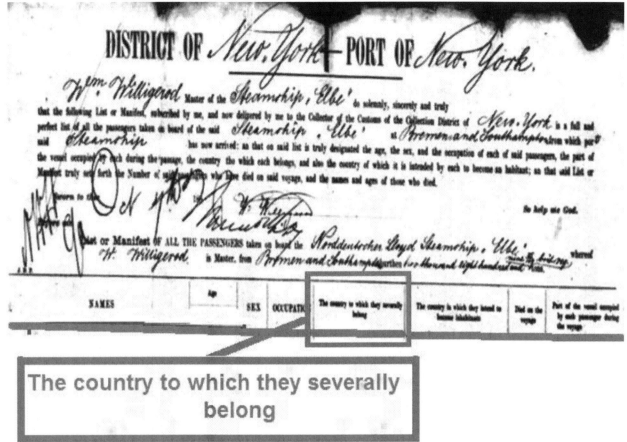

The country to which they severally belong

Five possible sources for Passenger Manifests

1.   **Ellisisland.org (New York only – 1892 & after)**

The Ellis Island Immigration Station opened on January 1, 1892 and had three large ships land on the first day with 700 immigrants passing through its gates. Almost 450,000 immigrants were processed at the station during its first year and about 1.5 million immigrants were processed through this immigration station in its first five years in use. However, on June 15, 1897, a fire possibly caused by faulty wiring, turned the wooden structures on Ellis Island into ashes. No losses of life were reported. However most of the immigration records dating back to 1855 were destroyed. The Barge Office was once again used as the immigration station while a new fireproof immigration station on Ellis Island was being built. The peak year for immigration at Ellis Island was 1907, with 1,004,756 immigrants processed. Note that Ellis Island was the largest and main immigration station but many European immigrants also arrived through the ports of Boston, Philadelphia, Baltimore, New Orleans and Canada. Passenger manifests from these other ports are not available through the Ellis Island website.

The Statue of Liberty-Ellis Island Foundation (SO LEIF) was founded in 1982 to restore the Statue of Liberty and Ellis Island.

The Foundation, working with its public partner, the National Park Service of the U. S. Department of the Interior, first restored and upgraded the Statue of Liberty. Work on the statue included restoring the outside finish of the statue after almost a century of weathering and pollution plus replacement of her torch and strengthening of her crown's rays. An army of architects, historians, engineers, and almost 1000 laborers also installed new elevators and an informative exhibit in the

Statue's base. The July 4th weekend, 1986, saw a gala three-day event celebrating the restoration.

The Foundation then turned its attention to the restoration of Ellis Island--the largest historical restoration in the history of the United States. The buildings of Ellis Island had sadly deteriorated over the years. When the Island re-opened in September of 1990--two years ahead of schedule-- it unveiled the world-class Ellis Island Immigration Museum, where some rooms appeared as they had during the height of immigrant processing. Other areas housed theaters, libraries, an oral history recording studio, and exhibits on the immigration experience. In the 1990s, the Foundation restored two more buildings (for a total of 5 buildings saved and restored on Ellis Island), expanding and upgrading the Museum Library and Oral History Studio, and creating a Children's Orientation Center and the Ellis Island Living Theatre. The Ellis Island Immigration Museum has welcomed nearly 40 million visitors since its opening in 1990.

Ellis Island Museum

Working to promote knowledge of the Island, the Statue, and immigration history, the Foundation has also published and made available to libraries and schools many books and curriculum guides, as well as a CD-ROM produced in collaboration with the History Channel.

The Foundation's current project is a significant expansion of the Ellis Island Immigration Museum to be called The Peopling of America® Center. The Center will enlarge the story currently told of the Ellis Island Era (1892-1954) to include the entire panorama of the American immigration experience from this country's earliest day's right up to the present. It is expected to be completed in 2012.

Passenger records for immigrants who were processed at Ellis Island are available for search and viewing at http://www.ellisisland.org/. The site states over 25 million records are available for viewing. To search you are required to register and a subscription is not required. Digital copies of the actual are available for viewing. However, there are no options available to download a digital copy although you should be able to do a screen print to save a copy. An 8 ½ x 11 archival quality certificate can be ordered from the Foundation for $29 and you may also order an 11 x 17 copy of each page for $29 per page or an 11 x 22 copy for $39 per page.

2. **CastleGarden.org – index (New York only – up to 1891**

Castle Garden was New York's first immigration station and it predated Ellis Island. It had more than 8 million people arrived through it's from 1855 to 1890.

Castle Garden – ca 1880

The Battery Conservancy created CastleGarden.org as an educational project. This is a free site that offers access to an extraordinary database of information on 11 million immigrants from 1820 through 1892. The site offers indexes and extractions of the information from the passenger manifests but does not offer digital copies of the actual documents. Below is an example of a page that shows the details available from the Castle Garden website. I have used the Castle Garden website to find the arrival information for some of my ancestors that I could not find on other internet databases. I then used the arrival information to find the digital copy of the document on Ancestry.com.

Sample page from CastleGarden.org

CHRISTIAN SCHULTZ			
FIRST NAME	CHRISTIAN	RELATIVE LEFT BEHIND	
LAST NAME	SCHULTZ	NAME OF RELATIVE LEFT BEHIND	
OCCUPATION	SUGAR BAKER	ADDRESS OF RELATIVE LEFT BEHIND	
AGE	23	TICKET	
SEX	Male	PAID BY	Self
LITERACY	Unknown	IN THE US BEFORE	Unknown
SHIP	SIR ROBERT PEEL	IN THE US WHEN	
ARRIVED	10 Mar 1849	IN THE US WHERE	
COUNTRY	SWEDEN	GOING TO SOMEONE IN THE US	Unknown
PORT OF DEPARTURE	LONDON	RELATIONSHIP TO THAT SOMEONE IN THE US	
PLACE OF LAST RESIDENCE	U	NAME OF RELATIVE IN THE US	
PROVINCE OF LAST RESIDENCE	UNKNOWN		
CITY OR VILLAGE OF DESTINATION	UNITED STATES	ADDRESS OF RELATIVE IN THE US	
PLAN	Unknown	CITY OF RELATIVE IN THE US	
PASSAGE	Unknown	COUNTRY OF BIRTH	SWEDEN
MONEY		PLACE OF BIRTH	

3. **Ancestry.com (All ports)**

 Ancestry.com is a subscription-based genealogy research website with over 5 billion records online and offers the largest selection of digital copies of passenger records. Documents from most ports of entry are available in the Ancestry.com databases. This includes arrivals from the major ports of New York, Philadelphia, Boston and Baltimore but also arrivals from Canadian ports and border crossings. This site can also be accessed at most libraries using Ancestry Library Edition. Below is shown the basic search page for Ancestry.com but more detail search screens are available if specific ports of entry are searched. Digital copies of the actual documents can be saved to your computer from Ancestry.com's databases. If you cannot find your ancestors using simple searches, you may need to use advance search methods by using name variations and wild cards. Also remember that documents were lost in the 1897 fire of the Ellis Island Building and that some documents were damaged due to their age.

Sample search page from Ancestry.com

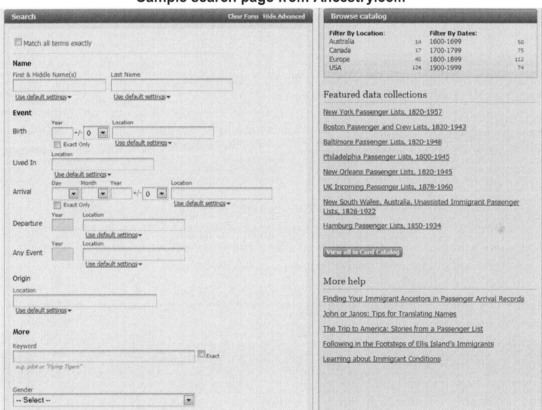

4. **Local libraries (search by date and ship)**

Before passenger records were available online, 35mm films that contained copies of the actual documents were purchased by some libraries to make this information available to their patrons. Each film was organized by date of arrival and by ship but no index of passengers was available. Each film has to be viewed page by page to find the name of your ancestors. These films are now rarely used due to the availability online of their images and because they are searchable online by the immigrant's name.

5. **National archives (All ports)**

Paper copies of original passenger manifests from 1820 to 1959 can be obtained from the National Archives at their website http://www.archives.gov/ for $25. If you visit one of the Regional National Archive sites, you can obtain a paper copy for the nominal copying cost. Below is a sample page used to order passenger records from the website. Note that you need to register for a free account before you can sign onto this order screen.

Sample Passenger Manifest Order Page at the National Archives website

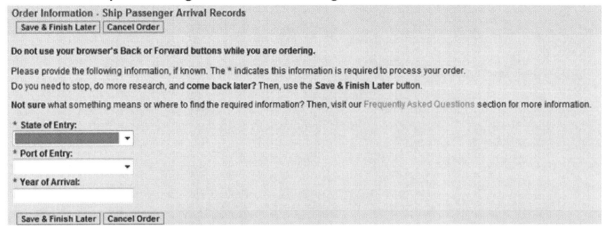

Order Information - Ship Passenger Arrival Records

[Save & Finish Later] [Cancel Order]

Do not use your browser's Back or Forward buttons while you are ordering.

Please provide the following information, if known. The * indicates this information is required to process your order.

Do you need to stop, do more research, and come back later? Then, use the Save & Finish Later button.

Not sure what something means or where to find the required information? Then, visit our Frequently Asked Questions section for more information.

* State of Entry:

* Port of Entry:

* Year of Arrival:

[Save & Finish Later] [Cancel Order]

Summary for Passenger Manifests

1. Passenger manifests may list birthplace and/or place of last
2. Passenger manifest information can be found at the National Archives (regional locations and online), some local libraries, Ancestry.com, Ellis Island website and Castle Gardens website
3. Copies of the actual manifest can be obtained from Ancestry.com, Ellis Island website, National Archives (online and regional locations) and some local libraries

• *Social Security Application*

The Social Security Act was signed into law by Franklin D. Roosevelt in 1935 to provide retirement income to workers in their old age. Employees were required to register for a Social Security card and number. This process required proof of their birthdates and the application will list not only their birthdates but also their place of birth and the names of their parents.

Below is shown the Social Security application of my grandfather. Note that his birthplace was written phonetically (Czyvef instead of Czyzew).

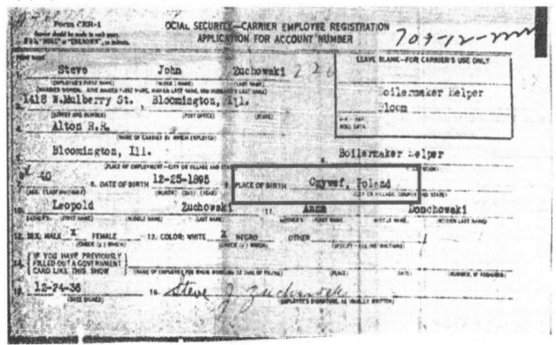

You can obtain a copy of a Social Security application for your ancestor by sending a letter to the Social Security Administration listing the name and social security number of your ancestor and a check. Below is a form letter that you can use to request a copy of the application.

Letter Requesting SS Application

Social Security Administration
OEO FOIA Workgroup
300 N. Green Street
P.O. Box 33022
Baltimore, Maryland 21290-3022

Please send me a photocopy of the actual application for a Social Security card (Form SS-5--Social Security Number Record Third Party Request for Photocopy) filed by the person listed below.

I obtained this information from the Social Security Death Master file at Ancestry.com, Inc. who obtained it from the Social Security Death Master file, originally compiled by the Social Security Administration.

My understanding is that the fee is $27, when the Social Security number is provided or $29 if the Social Security number is unknown or incorrect. Enclosed is a check or money order for $_____, made payable to the Social Security Administration.

Name of Person
Social Security Number
Birth Date
Death Date

Thank you for your assistance.

Sincerely,

Your Name
Your Address
Your Daytime Phone Number

Summary for the Social Security Application
1. The application process for a Social Security number required a document showing the date of birth for the applicant and the application also included a space for place of birth that was shown on the document of birth.
2. Using the Social security Death Index on Rootsweb.com, you can request a copy of the application by using the form letter provided by the Social Security Administration and paying $27 or $29.

- *Military Records*

The military records that I found the most useful were World War II draft registrations which usually listed the town of birth for foreign born registrants. One format of the World War I draft registration also is useful. Three formats of World War I draft registration cards were used and the last format used listed town of birth but the first two did not. Another possible military source would be found if immigrants fought in the revolutionary War and the Civil War. Their pension applications due to their service in these two conflicts may list their birthplace.

The above records are available online at:

- WW II draft registrations cards - Ancestry.com, Fold3.com (Subscription websites but usually available on local library databases) and Family Search.org
- WW I draft registration cards - Ancestry.com and Fold3.com (Subscription websites but usually available on local library databases)
- Revolutionary War pension applications - Heritage Quest (usually available on local library databases)
- Civil War pension index cards - Ancestry.com, Fold3.com (Subscription websites but usually available on local library databases) and Family Search.org

Below are two examples of the World War I and World War II draft registrations that list some useful information of ancestor's birthplaces. Also remember that the WW I draft registrations used three different formats and only the last one listed place of birth. The town names given on these two documents should be accurate because it was given by the person who was born there. Again use these names as clues to help locate the area and note that the town name that is given may be a misspelling.

WW I draft registration

WW II draft registration

REGISTRATION CARD—(Men born on or after April 28, 1877 and on or before February 16, 1897)

SERIAL NUMBER	1. NAME (Print)		ORDER NUMBER
U.1542	John Chmielewski		
	(First) (Middle) (Last)		

2. PLACE OF RESIDENCE (Print)

45 Ash St., Jersey City,   Hudson, N.J.
(Number and street)   (Town, township, village, or city)   (County)   (State)

[THE PLACE OF RESIDENCE GIVEN ON THE LINE ABOVE WILL DETERMINE LOCAL BOARD JURISDICTION; LINE 2 OF REGISTRATION CERTIFICATE WILL BE IDENTICAL]

3. MAILING ADDRESS

Same
[Mailing address if other than place indicated on line 2. If same insert word same]

4. TELEPHONE	5. AGE IN YEARS	6. PLACE OF BIRTH
None	47	Czuzuw (Town or county)
(Exchange) (Number)	DATE OF BIRTH 12 - 24 - 1894 (Mo.) (Day) (Yr.)	Poland (State or country)

7. NAME AND ADDRESS OF PERSON WHO WILL ALWAYS KNOW YOUR ADDRESS

Mrs. Stella Chmielewski - 45 Ash St.

8. EMPLOYER'S NAME AND ADDRESS

Lehigh Valley Railroad

9. PLACE OF EMPLOYMENT OR BUSINESS

Washington St.,   Jersey City, Hudson, N.J.
(Number and street or R. F. D. number)   (Town)   (County)   (State)

I AFFIRM THAT I HAVE VERIFIED ABOVE ANSWERS AND THAT THEY ARE TRUE.

John Chmielewski
(Registrant's signature)

D. S. S. Form 1
(Revised 4-1-42)   (over)   16-21630-1

Revolutionary War and Civil War pension applications usually list the birthplace of the applicant and will usually list the country of birth for an immigrant but sometimes will list the town of birth also. Since documentation of the birthplace for immigrants from these time periods are rare, reviewing these pension papers may be useful. Revolutionary War pension applications are in narrative format and are available at HeritageQuestOnline which is available on most local library databases. Civil War pension card indexes are available at Ancestry. Com, Fold3.com and Familysearch.org.

Note on Military Service Records

Military service records normally will list the birth place for the service man in their enlistment papers. The enlistment papers would be included in the personnel files stored at the National Personnel Records Center in St Louis, Missouri. However, if your ancestor was in the Army or Army Air Corp/Air Force, their records were probably destroyed in a 1973 fire. Personnel at the National Archives are trying to reconstruct some of the files by building consolidated files for each military personnel from documents that were stored in files at other locations. This requires searching all military files that were not in the St Louis Records Center at the time of the file and trying to find documents that pertain to individuals and then placing copies of these documents in new files for the individuals. This will not replace all of the facts contained in the files that were burned but hopefully capture some facts of the service of personnel that were affected by the fire.

Navy records were not burned in the fire and are available.

After initially being told the files of my father and grandfather were destroyed, I was able to obtain copies of parts of the files for my father (WW II) and grandfather (WW I) through a request to my congresswoman. The copies that I received were those recovered by the National Archives personnel and were stored at the National Archives. To obtain the copies from the National Archives, I had to pay a $60 fee to cover the cost of the copies and processing.

The first illustration shown below is the WW I enlistment page for my grandfather. There is a space to list his birthplace and it listed Russia as the country but the name of his village cannot be read because it has faded. Notice the black edges that were damaged in the fire.

The page in my grandfather's enlistment papers that listed his place of birth

Sources for Military records:

- **Family Search Record Search** - Free. Includes *Civil War Pension Index Cards* (no images), Louisiana War of 1812 Pension Lists (images only), World War II Draft Registration Cards, 1942 (images only), Vermont Enrolled Militia records, 1861-1867 (images only). Civil War Soldiers and Sailors System. Free National Park Service site with a nationwide index to Union and Confederate servicemen, including U.S. Colored Troops (USCT).
- **HeritageQuestOnline -** Search selected records from the Revolutionary War era pension and bounty-land warrant application files. This subscription site is also available at selected libraries.
- **Ancestry.com** - A subscription site with records from most major American wars, including DAR Rolls of Honor, the Civil War Collection, and World War I Draft Registrations. Also includes selected Loyalist and Confederate sources.
- **Fold3.com** - (formerly Footnote) Subscription site that has digitized and indexed National Archives documents including Civil War Service Records, Civil War Widows Pensions, Mormon Battalion Pension Files, Pension Index-Civil War to 1900, Revolutionary War Pensions, Southern Claims Commission, WWI and WWII records.

Summary for Military Records

1. WW II and some WWI draft registration cards will list birthplaces.
2. Military enlistment documents should include the birthplace of the enlistee
3. Most U.S. Army and Air Force records were destroyed in a 1973 fire and are not available.

• **Employment/Retirement Records**

If available, employment records usually include the place of birth of the workers. These job application forms required listing their place of birth and this form would have been saved in the main file for the employee. However, I have found that very few employment records are available for genealogy research due to privacy issues and the fact that most corporations do not have the personnel to retrieve the files for your research.

What is available:

Retirement papers for all railroad employees

I have found that the retirement files for railroad employees are available from the Railroad Retirement Board (RIB). Legislation was enacted in 1934, 1935, and 1937 to establish a railroad retirement system. RRB administers the pensions of all railroad employees from all companies and their records are separate from the social security program that was legislated in 1935. Their files include not only the employee's pension applications but also numerous papers concerning service dates and in some case the amount of pay. Marriage and insurance information may also be included.

For more information on requesting genealogical information from the Railroad Retirement Board go to their Genealogy Research web page at : http://www.rrb.gov/mep/genealogy.asp. Your request and payment of $27 fee will give you copies of all papers in their files. Allow about 30-60 days for the RRB to find the files and send you copies.

Below is a copy of a page from my grandfather's railroad retirement file that lists his birthplace.

Pullman-Standard Employment Records

Pullman-Standard was the leading producer of railroad passenger cars in the early 1900s. The company also played a leading role as an arsenal during WW I and WW II when it produced freight cars, tanks, and munitions for America's war efforts during both World Wars. Thousands of employees from Northwest Indiana and Chicago contributed to the success of Pullman-Standard at their Hammond, Michigan City, and Chicago locations. Since employees routinely transferred within the Pullman-Standard plants located in Indiana and Illinois, information on a particular employee may be scattered between sources in Indiana and in Illinois

I found that the South Suburban Genealogical Society (SSGS) in Crestwood, Illinois was able to save the personnel files for the employees from the now closed Pullman Standard Car Works plant in Chicago, Illinois. In 1982, the Society somehow was able to save employment files that cover the period from about 1900 through World War II and account for approximately 152,000 Pullman employees. Prior to South Suburban taking possession of the records, they had been stored in a wood kiln in Hammond, Indiana. In January of 1983, the SSGS started alphabetizing more than a million Pullman employment documents (they were previously kept in numerical order). It took six years and 2,560 volunteer hours to clean, re-box, and index this massive collection. The files may also include many personal papers such as birth certificates. The Pullman collection is not open to the public. Research is done only by authorized volunteers. SSGS staff will search the Pullman files at no charge to find if your ancestor is in the records but there is a fee if you order a copy of the file. The efforts of the South Suburban Genealogical Society are just one example of what files may be available.

The Calumet Regional Archives holds the employee records for the Pullman Car Works in Hammond, Indiana. These records have been cataloged by volunteers from the Northwest Indiana Genealogical Society and the index can be searched on the NWIGS website at:

http://www.rootsweb.ancestry.com/~innwigs/ using their Online Archives and/or Research Resources page.

More Pullman employee records can be found at the Newberry Library in Chicago which has the files for the Pullman car service employees (such as Porters, etc).

Other employment records
The Chicago and Northwestern Historical Society is another source for employee records because their holdings include the files for the employees of Chicago & Northwestern Railroad.

Another group of employee records to explore would be those of union workers. You will probably not be able to get the employee records from the company where they worked but the union my allow access to the records that show dues payments by their members and the union pension boards may release the pension files for your ancestor.

More employment records from defunct companies may have been saved by local genealogy or historical groups. As an example, I found the employee cards from the Gary Screw and Bolt Company listed on the NWIGS web site. Most records for defunct companies were destroyed when their offices were cleared out. However, try contacting local societies where your ancestor worked to see if they have any employment records for local companies - you may find a treasure. Note this is not true for companies that were merged or purchased since the files of the old company would have been merged into the new company.

Summary for Employment Records
1. Employment records should list place of birth.
2. However, most employments records may not be available due to privacy concerns and due to the fact that older files would be stored in archives and not available for public viewing.
3. The Railroad Retirement Board does offer copies of the files for their retirees for a search fee.
4. Also some genealogy societies and libraries have been able to save the personnel files for some defunct companies and these would be available for genealogical research.

• Death Records
Death records such as death certificates and obituaries for immigrants sometimes list a birthplace but you should be concerned with the accuracy of the information on these documents.

1. Many times the record only lists the country.
2. Many times the birth place is listed as "unknown" on death certificates.
3. The information may be wrong because the information was given by someone who did not know or remember the correct information.
4. If the death certificate or obituary lists a birthplace, use it as a place name to include on your list of clues but remember that it may be the least accurate.

In order to judge the accuracy of the information on death records, review the death certificate for the name of the informant. The information may be accurate if the informant was also born in the same birth place. If the informant was one of the children who were born after immigration, the information should be used carefully and the place name given may be a phonetic spelling.

Below are some examples of death certificates that I found useful in identifying the birthplaces of ancestors.

Below is the death certificate for Waleryan Puchalski. It lists the town of Glebokie, Poland as his birthplace. The informant on the certificate was his wife Mary who he met and married in Chicago, Illinois. Since Mary was not born in the same area as Waleryan, Glebokie is probably the phonetic spelling of his birthplace. This was the only document found for Waleryan that listed a town for his birthplace. The only other clue of where he was born was that Russia was listed on the 1900 and 1910 census records. I found fifteen different locations that could be variations of the Glebokie name but only three were in areas that were part of Russia in 1910. I also used the fact that his occupation was a shoemaker to find his birth record in the village of Hlybokae in present day Belarus which had a shoemaker school.

Death certificate for Waleryan Puchalski

Below is the death certificate for Elizabeth Szabados, my grandmother. Her birthplace is listed as Erdo Hegy, Hungary which was given accurately by her husband Erwin Szabados. Although my grandparents met after they immigrated, Erdo Hegy is located near where my grandfather was born. He would have been familiar with the town and should have been able to give an accurate place of birth for his wife.

Death certificate for Elizabeth Szabados

Obituaries

Many obituaries give only the name of the person who died, the names of their spouse and children and other surviving members of his family.

Occasionally some families give many more details. A more detailed obituary is a good source for information about a person. It gives the name of the deceased and the death or burial date. It may also contain information such as the birth date, place of birth, marriage date, names of parents and spouse, children, occupation, education, and the location of living family members at the time the obituary was written.

Below are three obituaries that list where the decedent was born in the old country. Two of them list when they arrived in the United States.

Below is the obituary for my grandmother Josephine Szabados. The information was given to the funeral director by her daughter who was born in America. Also alive and attending the funeral, were her two sons who were also born in Pankota and another daughter who was born in America. Josephine's marriage record listed Apatin as her birthplace. Her children assumed Pankota was her birthplace because this was their last residence before emigration and two of the children were born in Pankota.

Obituary for My grandmother Josephine Szabados

Bloomington- Normal Deaths

Mrs. Josephine Szabados

Mrs. Josephine Szabados, 76, of 1308 Northwestern Ave. died in the family residence at 2:30 p. m. Wednesday after an illness of two months.

She was taken to the Carmody Funeral Home and will be returned to the residence Thursday afternoon at four o'clock. Services will be held in the residence at 8:30 a. m. Saturday and in St. Mary's Church at 9 a. m. Burial will be in St. Joseph's Cemetery.

Mrs. Szabados was born March 19, 1877 in Pankota, Hungary, the daughter of John and Suzanne Zerna. She was married to Martin Szabados in 1891 in Hungary and came to the United States and to Bloomington in 1907.

Her husband, two daughters, one brother and seven sisters preceded her in death.

Surviving children are Ervin of Roodhouse, Fred of Peoria, Mrs. Maria Westerdahl of 1311 N. Livingston St. and Mrs. Suzanne Myers of 1308 Northwestern Ave. Also surviving are seventeen grandchildren and five great grandchildren. Mrs. Szabados was a member of St. Mary's Church, the St. Anne Society and the Catholic Order of Foresters.

Szabados Funeral

Funeral services for Mrs. Josephine Szabados, 76, of 1308 N. Western Ave., were held at 8:30 a. m. Saturday at the family home and at 9 a. m. at St. Mary's Church. Burial was in St. Joseph's Cemetery. Mrs. Szabados died Wednesday.

The Rev. Fr. Aloys Schweitzer celebrated requiem high mass. The Rev. Fr. John Ring was deacon and the Rev. Fr. Madian Schneider was sub-deacon. Father Schweitzer delivered the funeral sermon and officiated at the graveside.

St. Anne's Society formed an honorary escort. Pallbearers were Martin Szabados, Jesse Szabados, Louis Magy, Martin Deutsch Jr., Joseph Kober and John Szepcsik.

Below is the obituary for Bertha Pohl Lutz who was the great aunt for my daughter-in-law. The obituary lists her birthplace, immigration plus her living brothers and sisters. Since her brothers and sisters also immigrated as teens or adults, the birthplace that is listed is probably accurate and I have found the town on a map. This is a great obituary for the genealogist because it not only gives her birthplace but it also gives a short history of her life from the time she left Germany, her marriage and includes a list of moves she made with her husband and family.

1942 Obituary for Bertha Pohl Lutz
Obtained from Calhoun County Genealogy Society

Rites for Mrs. Lutz Held Last Saturday

Mrs. Bertha Lutz was born July 1, 1877 at Buchfelde, Province of Posen, Germany. In 1882 the family left the old home and country and came to the United States, where they found a new home at Varna, Ill.

On the 18th day of April, 1895, Bertha Pohl was married to Ernest Lutz, at Winona, Ill. This union was blessed with seven children, of whom two preceded their mother in death. For more than 47 years Mr. and Mrs. Lutz were permitted to share the joys as well as the toils and care of life together.

They moved to Sheldon, Ia., in 1896, where they lived until 1902, when they moved to Manson. In 1913 the family moved to near Clare and in 1919 to Terril; in 1931 they returned to Manson and made their home in the country northeast of town.

Mrs. Lutz enjoyed good health most of her life, which enabled her to attend to the manifold duties of a faithful wife and mother. Last winter she began to suffer from a complication of ailments, but recovered sufficiently to assume her household duties. About two weeks ago she became seriously ill with heart trouble, yet she overcome this attack sufficiently to be able to leave her bed for a short time. On Wednesday morning of last week she suffered another attack, and fell peacefully asleep that afternoon.

Mrs. Lutz leaves to mourn her departure, her aged husband, three sons, Arthur of Terril, Edward of Manson and George of Barnum, two daughters, Margaret, Mrs. Carl Suhrbier of Pocahontas and Irene, Mrs. Walter Weber of Dickens, Ia.; 14 grandchildren, three great-grandchildren, two brothers, Gustave Pohl of Jeffers, Minn., and Adolph Pohl of Rolfe, Iowa.

The funeral service was held at Williams Funeral home on Saturday, June 6, with the Rev. W. E. F. Meier officiating, and the body laid to rest in Roes Hill cemetery.

The next obituary shown below is the obituary for Josef Joza from the Czech language newspaper Denni Hlasatel. It listed his birthplace as Cerma near Susice in Bohemia (Čechy). There are a number of towns with the name of Cerma but only one near the town of Susice. This is a great obituary for the genealogist because it also lists Josef's parents and siblings plus the family members of his wife.

Obituary for Josef Joza - panel
From Denni Hlasatel February 22, 1912

Ordering a death certificate

To order a death certificate or find an obituary, you will need to know when your ancestor and their relatives died. Listed below are sources that may tell you when your ancestor died.

- **Social Security death index**

  The Social Security Act of 1933 required all employees to register with the Social Security Administration and to contribute along with their employers to the Social Security Fund. If they received any benefits before they died their death would be reported to the Social Security registration to stop the benefits and their death would be listed in the Social Security Death Index (SSDI). The SSDI can be searched at a number of sites online but I have found that Ancestry.com and Familysearch.org have been very useful.

- **State death indexes**

  If your ancestors are not listed in the SSDI, you may find them in a state death index that is based on death certificates that were recorded in state or county records. Some of these indexes may be found online at Ancestry.com and Familysearch.org. Also some states such as Missouri, Illinois, Wisconsin, Michigan, Minnesota, North Dakota, Ohio and Washington have their own websites with death indexes. Below is shown the Website for Minnesota deaths between 1904 and 2001.

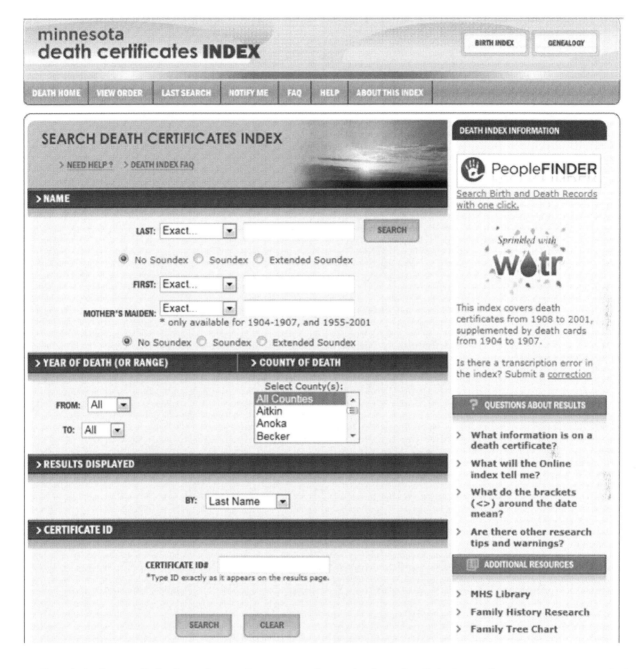

- **Death indexes listed on Ancestry.com** – Ancestry has death indexes for many states and also many indexes for churches and counties in the databases that they offer.
- **Death indexes listed on Familysearch.org** – Familysearch is digitizing and indexing their films and have many death records already uploaded with continuing plans to add more. Check this website regularly as they add databases monthly.

Cemetery records and grave stones

If you know the cemetery where your ancestors were buried, a trip to the cemetery should give you the date or at least the year of death by viewing the grave marker. Before you try to find the grave site, visit the cemetery office to obtain the location of the grave and a map of the cemetery – the person in the office may be able to mark the location on the map. If you live too far away from the cemetery to visit, you may be able to call the cemetery office and get the date of burial. If the name of the cemetery is not known, searching a number of nearby cemeteries may locate the grave site but will be more time consuming. Many local genealogy societies have also compiled cemetery books that list all burials by cemetery. On the following sample page notice the extra information listed about relationships plus the listing of parents in some cases.

Sample page from St Joseph's Cemetery, Bloomington, Illinois

```
ST. JOSEPH'S CEMETERY PAGE- 41
 CS     KERNER      Frank      no dates        hus. of Josephine
                    Josephine (Mayer)  Feb. 16, 1868 - July 9, 1936
                       wife of Frank
                       dau. of Joseph MAYER
                    Theresa  (Kerner) FOLKS
 SS                 FRANK    May 21, 1903 -                 hus. of Eva
                    Eva (Hirsch)  Dec. 24, 1903 -
                       wife of Frank
                    Frank J.   Dec. 7, 1931 - Dec. 14, 1973
                       Ill. EN2 US Navy Korea
                       son of Frank & Eva  ( Hirsch)
 CS                 Katherina (Kerner) HOFFMAN
 SS                 Lena (Kerner) MAYER
 CS                 Simon  Feb. 21, 1860 -Jan. 26, 1950   hus. of Theresa
                       son of John & Magdalena (Mueller)
                    Theresa (Takaes)  May 17, 1863 - May 30, 1941
                       wife of Simon
                       dau 6f Joseph & Theresa (Hubner) TAKAES
                    Simon, Jr.   Oct. 26, 1884 - Oct. 23, 1972  hus. of Magdalena
                       son of Simon & Theresa (Takaes)
                    Magdalena (Marksteiner) 1890 -
                       wife of Simon, Jr.
                       dau. of John & Anna (Foote) MARKSTEINER
                    Antoinette J.  1922-
                       dau. of Simon & Magdalena (Marksteiner) Jr.
 SS                 Rose C. (Kerner) EMERY
```

If you do not know the cemetery where your ancestors are buried, you may try using the online database at Findagrave.com. This is a free resource where you can search over 67 million grave records.

Funeral cards

Another source that will produce the date of death would be funeral cards that were circulated at the time of the funeral. These may be found in personal papers and scrap books of relatives. Be sure to ask all relatives about them. The cards may have been collected and saved by their parents.

Note that this funeral card not only lists the date of his death but also the birth date and cemetery. It also shows a stamp for the funeral home.

Sample back of funeral card

Eternal rest grant unto him O Lord, and let perpetual light shine upon him.

In your Charity

Pray for the repose of the soul of

Louis L. Weinberg

Oct. 25, 1892   March 21, 1984

Funeral Mass Held at

ST. IGNATIUS CHURCH

March 24, 1984   11:00 A.M.

Interment

ALL SAINTS CEMETERY

✝

Absolve we beseech Thee, O Lord, the soul of Thy departed servant that being dead to this world he may live to Thee, and whatever sins he may have committed through human frailty, do Thou, of Thy most merciful goodness forgive, through Jesus Christ Our Lord. Amen.

Our Father. Hail Mary.

JOHN E. MALONEY FUNERAL HOME

CROCE   © ⚓

PRINTED IN ITALY

Where to Obtain Death Certificates

- State Archives or Genealogy Societies
  Death certificates must be ordered from the State Health Departments in most states. The death certificates for some states are also available from state genealogical or historical societies. Check the websites of the state Genealogical society where your ancestor died to see if the offer copies of death certificates. Some states are also offering digital copies of death certificates that can be downloaded immediately from their websites. Below is shown the search page for Missouri

Death Certificates. The websites will show the actual death certificate and will allow a free download of the image.

Missouri Death Certificate search page

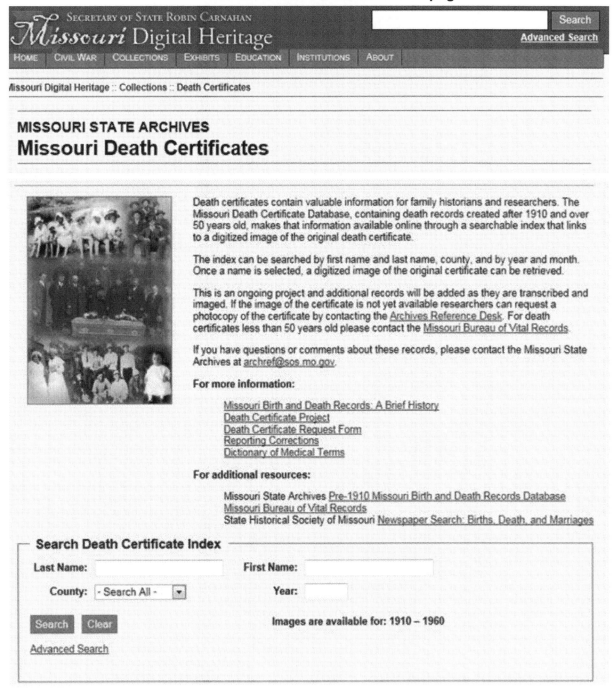

- **Family History Centers films**
  Death certificates are available on Family History Center films available on Famlysearch.org. Generally they are listed under the subject of vital records along with birth and marriage records. They will also be listed by county in date order.

**Webpage at Familysearch.org describing the
Illinois Death Certificates available on FHC Films**

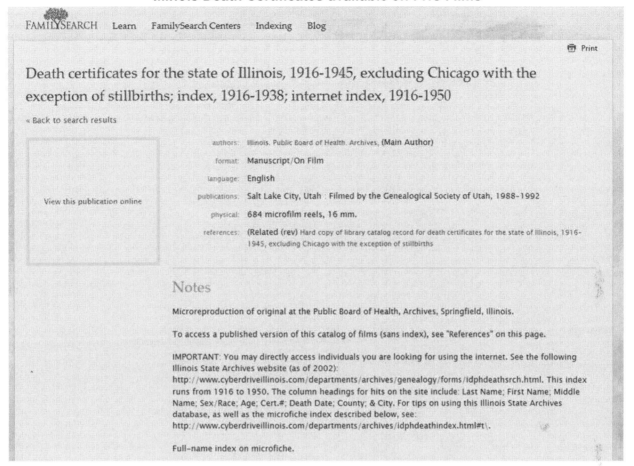

FAMILYSEARCH   Learn   FamilySearch Centers   Indexing   Blog

🖨 Print

Death certificates for the state of Illinois, 1916-1945, excluding Chicago with the exception of stillbirths; index, 1916-1938; internet index, 1916-1950

« Back to search results

View this publication online

authors:	Illinois. Public Board of Health. Archives. (Main Author)
format:	Manuscript/On Film
language:	English
publications:	Salt Lake City, Utah : Filmed by the Genealogical Society of Utah, 1988-1992
physical:	684 microfilm reels, 16 mm.
references:	(Related (rev) Hard copy of library catalog record for death certificates for the state of Illinois, 1916-1945, excluding Chicago with the exception of stillbirths

Notes

Microreproduction of original at the Public Board of Health, Archives, Springfield, Illinois.

To access a published version of this catalog of films (sans index), see "References" on this page.

IMPORTANT: You may directly access individuals you are looking for using the internet. See the following Illinois State Archives website (as of 2002):
http://www.cyberdriveillinois.com/departments/archives/genealogy/forms/idphdeathsrch.html. This index runs from 1916 to 1950. The column headings for hits on the site include: Last Name; First Name; Middle Name; Sex/Race; Age; Cert.#; Death Date; County; & City. For tips on using this Illinois State Archives database, as well as the microfiche index described below, see:
http://www.cyberdriveillinois.com/departments/archives/idphdeathindex.html#t\.

Full-name index on microfiche.

**Webpage at Familysearch.org showing some of the
film numbers available for Illinois Death Certificates**

Film Notes

Note	Location	Film
INDEX. 1916-1938. Full name, alphabetical on 191 microfiches.	FHL US/CAN Fiche	6016862
[1916 Deaths] ADAMS County, Illinois-BOND County, Illinois, certificate nos. 1-1501	FHL US/CAN Film	1530531
[1916 Deaths] BOND County, Illinois-COLES County, Illinois, certificate nos. 1502-4375	FHL US/CAN Film	1530532
[1916 Deaths] COLES County, Illinois-COOK County, Illinois, certificate nos. 4375-6938	FHL US/CAN Film	1530530
[1916 Deaths] COOK County, Illinois-CUMBERLAND County, Illinois, certificate nos. 6939-9409	FHL US/CAN Film	1531026

- **County Clerks or Health Departments**
  Some states may allow you to order death certificates from the county clerk or health department. Check both State and county websites to see which is available. Below is the web page of the McLean County, Illinois Health Departments vital records order page as an example.

Web page to order Death certificate from McLean County Health Department.

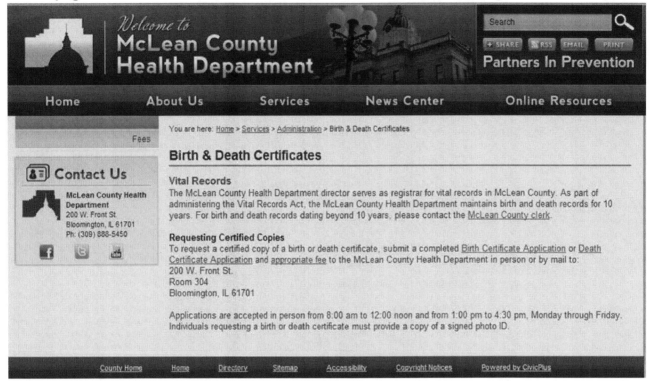

Where to find Obituaries

- **Online newspaper banks**
  There are many newspapers that have been digitized and are available online. In most cases most of their pages have are available online both news stories and obituaries. Most of these records are available at subscription websites but some are also available on your local library's online databases.

  Online Newspaper Archives websites are:
  - Newspaperarchive - http://www.newspaperarchive.com/
  - NewsBank - http://www.newsbank.com/
  - Genealogy Bank - http://www.genealogybank.com/gbnk/
  - Proquest - http://www.proquest.com/
  - Footnote – http://Footnote.com/
  - Godfrey Memorial Library - http://www.godfrey.org/

  You may also need to search the online archives for a small local paper that is not included on any of the large online databases. Go to their online website to do this search.

  Below is the search page for one of the online databases – NewsBank which offers obituaries from all states. This particular site offers options to select specific states and specific papers to limit your search and produce narrow search results. Most results for obituaries will be in a text format but some may be pictures of the newspaper pages.

Search page for NewsBank Obituaries available at many libraries

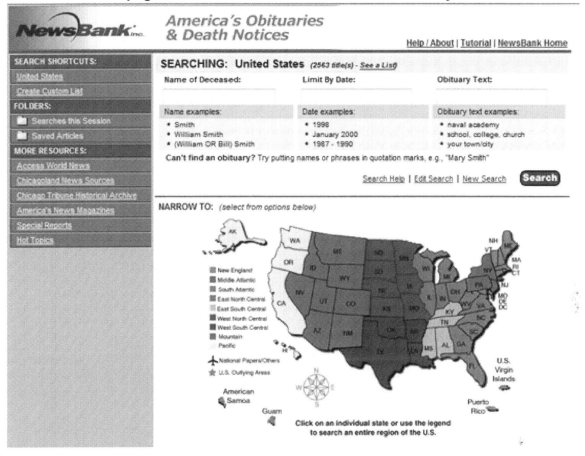

- ## Local genealogy or historical society collections

    Some local genealogical or historical societies may also have collections of obituaries that they have cutout and saved from their local papers. Societies may save these files at their local meeting room, their local library or their local historical museum. If their location is nearby you will find a visit will be very interesting. However, if their location is too distant for a day-trip, call, write or email them to find out what they have. If your list is small they will probably search their files and sent copies for a nominal fee or request for a donation.

Summary for Death records

1. Death certificates and obituaries may list place of birth
2. Towns listed of death records may be inaccurate but still should be used as clues.
3. To obtain a copy of the death certificate and obituary you will need to know when they died
4. Copies of the death certificate may be obtained from county offices and sometimes online
5. Copies of obituaries may be found on the internet at online news banks and also from local genealogical societies.

Your List of Place Names

You should now have a list of towns/villages that are somehow associated with your ancestors. Hopefully you found and reviewed all possible documents that may have a place name from where your ancestor left. Do not stop when you find the first name. Save all place names that you find. Your list may also include large cites near where your ancestor was born or the administrative district where they are locate. They will all help you find your ancestral home on a map.

.

Step Two - Learn the history of the Country/Area to narrow your Search

The next step in your search for your ancestors will require a review of the history of the country and various areas where your ancestor may have been born. Use history books, encyclopedias and town/county websites to do this. Also use various sources and compare the information found from each source - some will contain more detail than others.

The main objective is to study the histories for border changes. This will enable you to sort through the possible confusion of the country of birth on various documents for your immigrant ancestors. An example of this would be a 1900 census that may have listed that your Bohemian grandfather was born in Austria or your Polish grandmother was born in Russia. This is very important because all European countries have had border changes over the centuries. Check the borders of the country that existed at the time of the document. If you find that your ancestor came from an area that had border changes, you may narrow your search.

The following pages include maps that illustrate some of the border changes of Germany, Poland and the Austro-Hungarian Empire. I give these as examples of how border changes can be used to narrow your search for your ancestor's birthplace. If your ancestors immigrated from other areas, you need to research border changes of these areas. Your goal is to identify what the borders were at the time of the documents that list your ancestor.

German Border Changes

Let's start with the changes in Germany's borders that are pertinent to genealogy research.

German Confederation 1815-1866

The first illustration shows the map of the German Confederation that existed between 1815 and 1866. The confederation was formed by the Congress of Vienna in 1814 and was a loose league of 39 sovereign states. Many Germans immigrated to America during this period due to political pressures. The country listed on the US Federal Census records for 1850, 1860 and 1870 will list the country of birth as it existed on this map and should not be interpreted as another name for Germany. Using the name on the census and the borders of that country on the 1815-1866 map should narrow your search. If your ancestors listed one of the smaller states such as Coldberg or Oldenburg your search narrows quite a bit where as if they listed Preußen (Prussia) or Bayern (Bavaria) their search area is still very large. Note that the light area in the east represents Polish areas and these were added to the confederation in 1848 to 1851.

Map of the German Confederation (1815-1866) from the Wikimedia Commons media library

German Empire 1871 – 1918

Conflict between King William I of Prussia and the increasingly liberal parliament erupted over military reforms in 1862, and the king appointed Otto von Bismarck the new Prime Minister of Prussia. Bismarck successfully waged war on Denmark in 1864. The Prussian victory in the Austro-Prussian War of 1866 enabled him to create the North German Federation (Norddeutscher Bund) and to exclude Austria, formerly the leading German state, from the federation's affairs. After the French defeat in the Franco-Prussian War, the German Empire was proclaimed 1871 in Versailles, uniting all scattered parts of Germany except Austria (*Kleindeutschland*, or "Lesser Germany"). The colored areas shown on the map below were all included in the German Empire that existed between 1871 and 1918. The borders of the new German Empire would be listed on US census records for 1890, 1900 and 1910 as Germany. The

German Empire map is not as useful as the Confederation map because immigrants listed Germany as their country of birth and this represents a much larger area to search for their village.

Map of the German Empire (1871-1918) from the Wikimedia Commons media library

DAS DEUTSCHE REICH
1871-1918

Polish Border Changes

Understanding Polish border changes associated with the Polish Partitions and the changes after World War I is also very important in genealogy research.

Partitioning of Poland by Germany, Russia & Austria

Political movements within Poland to grant some democratic reforms led Poland's neighbors (Russia, Prussia and Austria) to partition Polish territory in 1772, 1793 and 1795. The chart to the right shows the territory that was partitioned by Russia, Prussia and Austria.

Throughout the period of the partitions, political and cultural repression of the Polish nation led to the organization of a number of uprisings against the authorities of the occupying Russian, Prussian and Austrian governments. Many Polish nobles had to leave Poland after Polish forces lost battles with the invading armies. Other Polish peoples who could afford to leave left in the early 1800s. Poles who emigrated in the late 1800s and the early 1900s were poor. They left because they could not find work or their farms were too small and their older brother would inherit.

The 1900 and 1910 US Census records for the Polish immigrants listed their country of birth as Germany, Russia or Austria. Many Polish immigrants were very proud of the Polish heritage and added Poland to the official country name and listed the country of birth as Poland-Germany or Poland-Russia or Poland-Austria. If the double name was not used, the researcher should check the language column on the 1910 Census record. If Germany, Russia or Austria were listed and the census record listed that the immigrant spoke Polish, then this would narrow the area of your search.

Map of the Partitions of Poland from the Wikimedia Commons media library

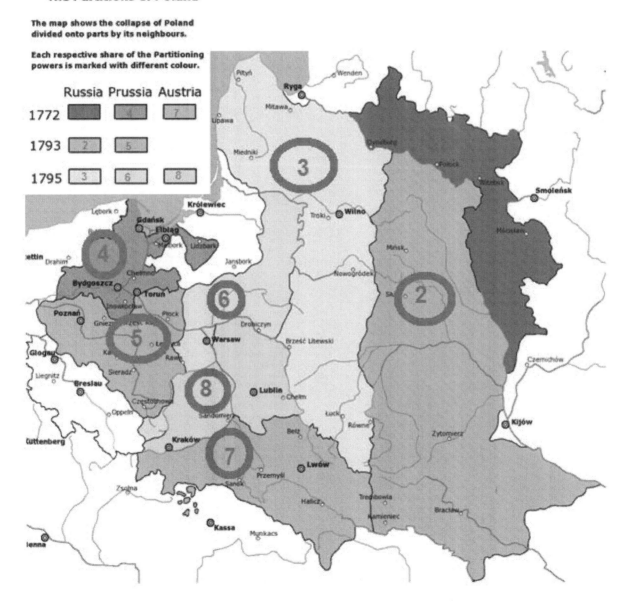

Post WW I Polish Borders

The end of World War I enabled the nationalist movements in many countries to gain legal support to break down the borders of the German Empire, the Austro-Hungarian Empire and Russia. Many new republics were formed. In Poland, a number of events during this time drastically reshaped the borders to what the new Republic of Poland was between 1919 and 1939.

- The December 27, 1918 Great Poland Uprising liberated Greater Poland.
- The Polish-Soviet war began in 1919 and victories by Polish forces gave Poland much of the Ukraine and what is Belarus today.
- The 1919 Treaty of Versailles settled the German-Polish borders in the Baltic region.
- Allied arbitration set German-Polish borders in Silesia.
- The port city of Gdansk with strong ties to both Poland and Germany was declared a "Free City"

Reviewing the 1910 and 1920 US census records for Polish immigrants should show different countries of birth and these differences will be clues in your search for your ancestor's birthplace because the differences will help narrow your search area.

Map of the Poland (1918-1939) from the Wikimedia Commons media library

Below is a map showing the 1937 linguistic distribution within Poland. Note that the eastern areas won by Poland in the 1919 Polish-Soviet War have very low distribution of Polish speaking inhabitants. This fact is very important when you look at the next map that shows the lands that were transferred to the Soviet Union after World War II. Although this map will not give any additional information in your Polish genealogical search for birthplaces, it will help with understanding why Poland lost its land in the Ukraine and Belarus after WW II.

Map showing the 1937 Linguistic Distribution of Poland Map
from the Wikimedia Commons media library

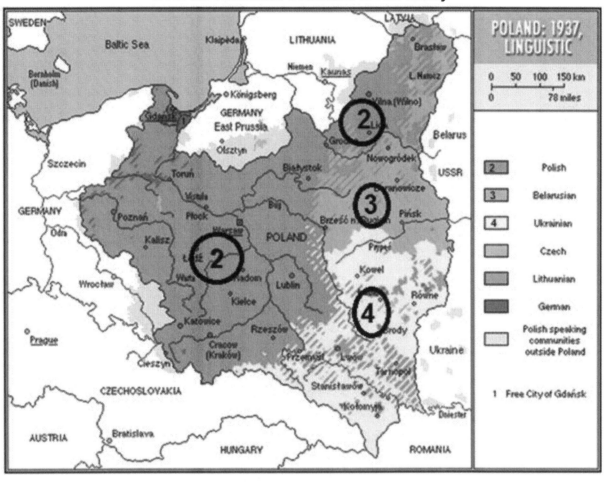

Map of the Poland after WW II from the Wikimedia Commons media library

1	annexed by Poland in 1945
2	annexed by Soviet Union in 1945

THE CURZON LINE

Break-up of the Austro-Hungarian Empire

Austro-Hungarian Empire 1910
Austria-Hungary (also known as the Austro-Hungarian Empire) was a constitutional monarchic union between the crowns of the Austrian Empire and the Kingdom of Hungary. The union was a result of the Austro-Hungarian Compromise of 1867, under which the House of Habsburg agreed to share power with the separate Hungarian government, dividing the territory of the former Austrian Empire between them. The territory of the Austrian Empire was inhabited by many ethnic groups that included Polish, Czech, Slovaks, Serbs, Germans, Hungarians, Ukrainians, Slovenes, Romanians, Italians and Croats. The Austrian and the Hungarian lands became independent entities enjoying equal status. The dual monarchy had existed for 51 years when it dissolved on 31 October 1918 before a military defeat in the First World War. As a result of treaties signed after World War I, Poland, Romania, and Italy gained lands

that were once ruled by Austria and Hungary. Also the countries of Yugoslavia, and Czechoslovakia were born. Austria and Hungary lost much of their territory and became much smaller separate countries.

Compare the two maps below and note that the borders for the new countries matched closely the ethnic distribution of the population of those lands. Also note that the German populations within Hungary and Transylvania were due to recruitment of new settlers by the Empress of Austria in the 1700 & 1800s for her frontier areas.

Map of the ethnic groups of Austria-Hungary 1910 from the Wikimedia Commons media library

Map of the Breakup of Austria & Hungary from the Wikimedia Commons media library

How border changes in Europe affected U.S. Federal census records.

Below is a comparison showing the birth country listed for immigrants in the 1910 and 1920 U.S. Federal records. This comparison shows how understanding the changes in European borders after WW I should clear up any confusion you may have had about the country where your ancestors were born. The birthplace for your ancestor did not change from the 1910 census to the 1920 census but really only the borders changed. Also note that these border changes will also narrow your search for the birthplace on a map.

1910 Census	1920 Census
Russia	Poland
Germany	Poland
Austria	Poland
Austria	Czechoslovakia
Austria	Yugoslavia
Austria	Italy
Austria-Hungary	Czechoslovakia
Austria-Hungary	Romania

County Histories

Another tool to use is the county websites in the areas that include some of the town names that you have found.

Most counties (Gminas) in Poland have websites. (Some counties in other counties also have websites.) These county websites are generally used as a communication tool for current county business and news. However, most counties also have pages that give a short account of their history and most have galleries of vintage pictures. All are very useful in determining which county was the birthplace of your ancestor. There may be facts in the histories or pictures that match information from other documents or from oral history that can narrow your search.

Also note that all of these websites will appear at first in the language of the country but your web browser may allow you to have the page translated. Below are two sample WebPages for Andrzejewo County in Poland. The first is in Polish and second page has been translated to English.

Andrzejewo County Web Page (in Polish)

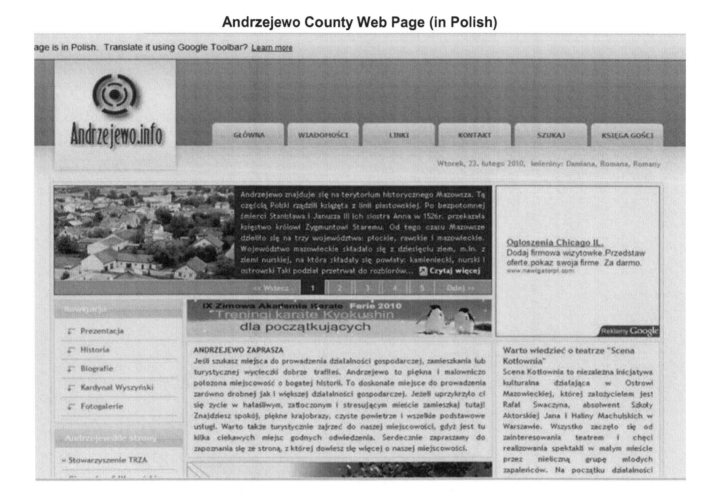

Andrzejewo County Web Page (in English)

An example of using county websites to help find a birthplace

Finding the birthplace for Waleryan Puchalski required some luck because I found only one document that included the name of a town. The death certificate for Waleryan Puchalski lists his birthplace as Glebokie, Poland and his occupation as shoe cobbler. The 1900 and 1910 census records listed that Waleryan was born in Russia.

Using his death certificate and census records, I was able to narrow my search to three villages. Research found 15 different towns that could be a variation of the Glebokie name. Only three of these towns were locate within the borders of Russia in 1900 and 1910.

I then got lucky when I researched the counties where these three villages were located and found an answer in the vintage pictures that I found on one of the county websites. The website for Hlybokaye, Belarus had a vintage picture of some young boys at a shoemaker's school. Although this did not definitely indicate that this was Waleryan's birthplace, it did give me a clue as where I should look further. When I ordered a film from the Family History Center for the birth records for this village, I found Waleryan. What Luck!!!

Below is the vintage picture from the website for Hlybokaye (Glubokaye in Polish) in Belarus showing young boys working at a school for shoemakers. After the picture is Waleryan's death certificate.

..

Shoemaker's Shop in Glubokoye (Hlybokaye), Belarus

Death certificate for Waleryan Puchalski

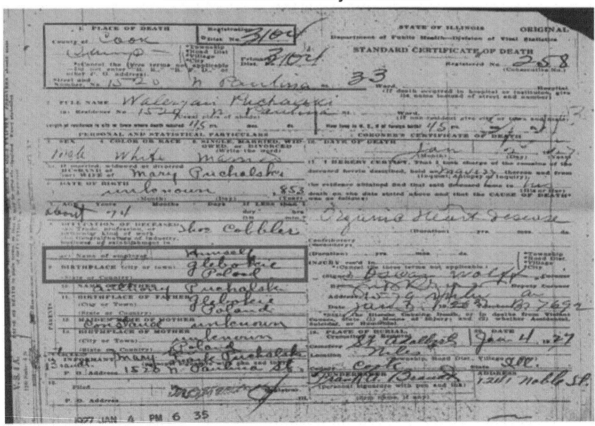

Border changes in other European countries

The above discussion covers the border changes in Germany and the East European countries that affect our genealogy research. Similar changes can be found in other European countries that can also furnish you clues that will narrow your search area for your ancestor's birthplace. Study the history of border changes in the country from where your ancestor left. You should study the years before and after your ancestor left and include all years that your documents cover.

Your Search

Hopefully your search will include more documents than my example of Waleryan Puchalski and not require the extreme luck that I experienced. Most of my research on my other ancestors yielded more documents and finding their birthplaces was more straight forward. The next section of this book discusses the use gazetteers that will help find the birthplace on a map.

Step Three - Use Gazetteers and maps to determine how clues fit together

Why use Gazetteers?

Gazetteers are very important to use when doing family history research because they help you pinpoint a specific place and associate towns with the jurisdictions to which they belong.

What is a Gazetteer?

A gazetteer is a dictionary of place names and is used in conjunction with a separate map. It is an important reference for information about places and place names. It typically contains information concerning the geographical makeup of a country, region, or continent as well as the social statistics and physical features, such as mountains, waterways, or roads. Gazetteers describe towns, villages, churches and states, rivers and mountains, populations, and other geographical features. They usually include only the names of places that existed at the time the gazetteer was published and often their former names. The place names are generally listed in alphabetical order, similar to a dictionary. They can also provide interesting facts about the community and help you to know where to look for additional records.

Gazetteers may also provide additional information about a town, such as its:
• Boundaries of civil jurisdiction.
• Longitude and latitude.
• Distances and direction from other from cities.
• Schools, colleges, and universities.
• Denominations and number of churches.
• Major manufacturing works, canals, docks, and railroad stations.

Gazetteers existed since the Hellenistic era in Greece. The first known gazetteer of China appeared by the 1st century, and with the age of print media in China by the 9th century, the Chinese gentry became invested in producing gazetteers for their local areas as a source of information as well as local pride. The earliest European gazetteer was written by geographer Stephanus of Byzantium who wrote a geographical dictionary in the 6th century which influenced later European compilers of gazetteers in the 16th century. Modern gazetteers can be found in reference sections of most libraries as well as on the Web.

Below I give the details of various gazetteers or websites for many of the European countries and a discussion on how to use them.

ShtetlSeeker Town Search (use first when searching for a village in a Eastern European country)

ShtetlSeeker and Town Locator is the search engine of the JewishGen website. It is based on the book *Where Once We Walked* compiled by noted genealogists Gary Mokotoff and Sallyann Amdur Sack and it uses the Daitch–Mokotoff Soundex system for approximate spellings of place names. It is a searchable catalogue of Jewish-populated locales in 19th – mid-20th century Central and Eastern Europe and features hot linked map coordinates. It is a very good website to use first when you have town names that you believe may have an incorrect spelling. It does not matter if that your family was not Jewish. It only maters that their village was located in the area that this database covers.

Below is the web page at **www.jewishgen.org/communities/loctown.asp**. Type in your town names in the search box and the results will usually list multiple towns that may be possible locations for your ancestors. Look for towns that match province and county information that you find. Locate each possible town on a map to see if the other town names that you found are close to one of the possible towns that are in the results list

Polish Gazetteers

The Slownik Geograficzny (Geographic Dictionary of the Former Kingdom of Poland and other Slavic Lands) is the commonly used gazetteer for Polish towns. The Slownik Geograficzny is a gazetteer that was published from 1880 to 1902 under the direction of Filip Sulimierski. It is an excellent gazetteer for locating places in the areas of Poland, both present and past. Coverage includes all localities in the former Polish provinces of Russia, most localities in the former Austrian province of Galicia (now divided between Poland and the Ukraine), Belorussian provinces of the Russian Empire (now in the Republic of Belarus), and also contains significant localities in other Slavic and eastern European nations; Russia, Slovakia, the Czech Republic, Hungary, Slovenia, Croatia, Serbia, Bulgaria and Romania. While the information is a bit less comprehensive, localities from the provinces of Poznan, West Prussia, East Prussia, Silesia, and Pomerania are also covered. The towns are listed alphabetical and the powiat (province) and gmina (county) is listed for each town.

Copies of the book are hard to find but CDs are available from the Polish Genealogical Society of America located in Chicago. Illinois. Ordering information can be obtained on the website at PGSA.org.

You can also view the gazetteer online at a new website at :

http://dir.icm.edu.pl/pl/Slownik_geograficzny/

You can also view the gazetteer online at a new website at :
http://dir.icm.edu.pl/pl/Slownik_geograficzny/

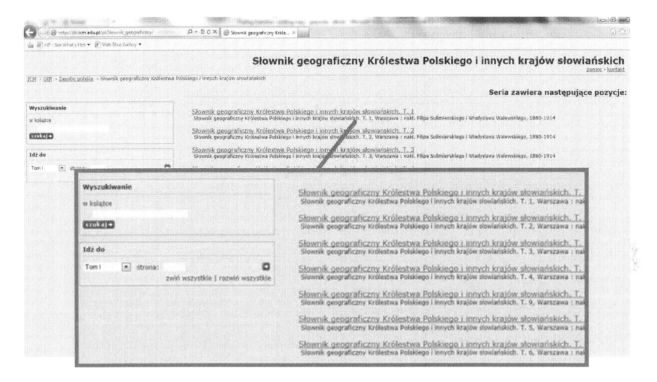

This Gazetteer has 16 volumes and the towns are listed alphabetically. Below is a list the towns by volume.

Vol No.	Town Names
1	Aa - Dereneczna
2	Derenek - Gzack
3	Haag - Ke~py
4	Ke~s - Kutno
5	Kutowa - Malczyce
6	Malczyce - Netreba
7	Netrebka - Perepia~t
8	Perepiatycha - Pozas~cie
9	Poz~as~cie - Ruksze
10	Rukszenice - Sochaczew
11	Sochaczew - Szlurbowska
12	Szlurpiszki - Warl~ynka
13	Warmbrunn - Worowo
14	Worowo - Z~yz~yn
15 part 1	Ababi - Janus (addendum)
15 part 2	Januszpol - Wola

Below is the Slownik Geograficzny listing for Przezdziecko Pierzchaly which is my grandmother's birthplace. I have also included a translation of the entire listing for Przezdziecko.

Translation of the entry for Prześdziecko from the Słownik Geograficzny
(by Brian Allen Wierzba at http://alsgenservice.com/)

Prześdziecko, nobility controlled area upon the Brok Mały River. Prześdziecko belongs to the County of Ostrowski, the District of Warchoły, and the Andrzejowo Parish. The nearest railway station is the Warszawa-St. Petersburg railway station, which is located between Czyżew and Ostrów. This slot of land (Prześdziecko) is inhabited by the Prześdziecki and Drogoszewski noble families.

Here are the villages that compromise Prześdziecko: 1) Prześdziecko Drogoszewo, this is now a peasant village. In 1827, there were 15 homes, with 90 inhabitants. See entry for Drogoszewo-Prześdziecko for more details. 2) Prześdziecko Dworaki, nobility owned village with 5 homes and 135 inhabitants. In 1827, there were 20 homes, with 118 inhabitants. 3) Prześdziecko Grzymki, a noble and peasant village, with 6 homes and 74 inhabitants. In 1866, the peasant land area totaled 13 morgs (14 settlements). The noble owned folwark had a land area totaling 336 morgs. In 1827, there were 10 homes, with 104 inhabitants.*

4) Przeździecko Jachy, in 1827, there were 12 homes, with 88 inhabitants. 5) Przeździecko Lenarty, in 1827, there were 9 homes, with 52 inhabitants. 6) Przeździecko Mroczki, in 1827, there were 9 homes, with 50 inhabitants. 7) Przeździecko Pierzchały, in 1827, there were 7 homes, with 58 inhabitants. The village is located between Przeździecko Jachy and Przeździecko Grzymki. The area is still known as Żale. There is an old cemetery along the coast of the Brok Mały River. As legend has it, the area was the site of a pagan temple, whose scattered large stones remain to this day. Among the numerous gentry families are the Pułazie and Załuski families.

German Sources

Meyer's Orts and Verkehrs Lexicon des Deutschen Reiches (Meyer's Directory of Places and Commerce in the German Empire 1912) by Dr. E Uetrecht is a gazetteer of the German Empire and is the best gazetteer to use to locate place names in German research. It was originally compiled in 1912. It is the best gazetteer to use because it includes all areas that were part of the pre-World War I (WWI) German Empire. Overall, this gazetteer includes more than 210,000 cities, towns, hamlets, villages, etc.

How to Use *Meyers Orts*:

Place names are listed alphabetically and are arranged in the following manner:
- Volume I: A-K
- Volume II: L-Z
- Volume III: Supplement (contains additions and corrections)

Each entry contains a paragraph of information. If all of the information is available it will include the following things and appear in the following order:
- Name of place
- Place type
- Name of state to which it belongs
- Government district
- Population
- Post Office and other Communications information
- Railroad information
- Courts
- Consulate
- Embassy
- Churches
- Schools
- Institutes
- Military
- Financial
- Business Institutions
- Trades and Industries
- Shipping Traffic
- Local government services
- Dependent Places

The paragraphs of information are full of abbreviations, which were used to save space. At the beginning of Volume I is an abbreviation list. This list will help you immensely in reading the entry.

Another difficult thing about using *Meyers Orts* is correctly deciphering the Gothic script that the work was printed in.

If your library does not have a copy of Meyers Orts on their shelves, you can use an electronic copy at Ancestry.com under the title: Meyers Gazetteer of the German Empire. Below is a portion of the page from Meyers Orts that shows the information for the town of Kalbe.

Meyer's Orts and Verkehrs Lexicon des Deutschen Reiches (sample section for the town of Kalbe)

Kartenmeister

Another online database to use to find your ancestor's German towns is Kartenmeister at **www.kartenmeister.com** This database contains 88813 locations and all locations are located east of the Oder and Neisse rivers. It includes towns within the borders of the eastern German provinces in the spring of 1918. Included in this database are the following provinces: Eastprussia (including Memel), Westprussia, Brandenburg, Posen, Pomerania, and Silesia. It currently lists most towns or points, points being, mills, some bridges, and battlefields. As more information becomes available, this database will be updated.

The database can be searched in several ways or criteria.
1. German name
2. Older German name
3. Kreis/County
4. By the next larger town, (this is a proximity search.)
5. Today's Polish, Russian or Lithuanian name.
6. by Family Name

Home page for www.Kartenmeister.com

 **DataBase**

[Home] [English] [Deutsch] [Polska] [Dictionary] [Latin-German-English] [Lithuanian-German-English] [Settlements] [Historic Background] [Kolonist] [Measurements.] [Border Changes] [Laws] [The Social Fabric] [Miscellanea] [Untitled]

There are 5 records that match your search criteria.

German Name	County
Louisenhof, Vorwerk	Schlawe
M"uhlbanz	Dirschau
Mihlbantz 1789	Dirschau
Milobadz 1789	Dirschau
Rosenberg	Neustettin

[Home] [English] [Deutsch] [Polska] [Dictionary] [Latin-German-English] [Lithuanian-German-English] [Settlements] [Historic Background] [Kolonist] [Measurements.] [Border Changes] [Laws] [The Social Fabric] [Miscellanea] [Untitled]

Hungary

Another example of an online gazetteer is the Radix website which lists the information from an 1882 gazetteer of Hungary. This gazetteer is based mainly on the national census of 1880 and came out in 1882. It can be viewed **at http://www.bogardi.com/gen/g104.shtml**. This gazetteer has two parts: the first part gives a listing of counties with their districts and settlements. Section two with the settlements sorted alphabetically has detailed information like number of houses, inhabitants, parishes, juridical and public administration affiliations of settlements. However, only section one is listed on this website. There are plans to add part two to the website sometime in the future.

Below is the web page that lists each county covered by the census. These include all counties of Hungary in 1880 even those that were lost to other countries after WW I. To find your ancestor's birthplace, click on each county listed below and review the list of towns shown for each county.

The list of counties

Abauj-Torna	Hajdu	Sopron
Alsó-Fehér	Háromszék	Szabolcs
Arad	Heves	Szatmár
Árva	Hont	Szeben
Bács-Bodrog	Hunyad	Szepes
Baranya	Jász-Nagy-Kun-Szolnok	Szilágy
Bars	Kis-Küküllő	Szolnok-Doboka
Békés	Kolozs	Temes
Bereg	Komárom	Tolna
Beszterce-Naszód	Krassó-Szörény	Torda-Aranyos
Bihar	Liptó	Torontál
Borsod	Máramaros	Trencsén
Brassó	Maros-Torda	Turóc
Csanád	Moson	Udvarhely
Csik	Nagy-Küküllő	Ugocsa
Csongrád	Nógrád	Ung
Esztergom	Nyitra	Vas
Fejér	Pest-Pilis-Solt-Kis-Kun	Veszprém
Fogaras	Pozsony	Zala
Gömör- és Kis-Hont	Sáros	Zemplén
Győr	Somogy	Zólyom

As an example, clicking on Arad, you will be able to review each town located in Arad county which is located in Transylvania and now a part of Romania. Below is a partial list of towns located in the old Hungarian county of Arad

Radix - 1882 gazetteer of Hungary

[return to description]

Mini dictionary: megye = county, székhely = seat, városok = towns (or cities), járás = district, szkv. = [szabad királyi város] = free royal town, tjv. = [törvényhatósági jogú város] = town with municipial rights, rtv. = [rendezett tanácsú város] = town with settled council, főváros = capital city
Legends: szkv-s, tjv-s, rtv-s are underlined, so-called nagyközség-s (large villages) are in *italic*

Arad megye

Székhely: Arad (szkv.)

Városok: Arad (szkv.)

Aradi járás
Székhely: Arad (szkv.)
Csicsér, Fakert, *Glogovác, Gyorok, Kurtics, Kuvin, Mácsa, Mikalaka*, Mondorlak, *Uj-Panát, Szabadhely, Szent-Leányfalva*, Szent-Pál, Zimánd-Ujfalu, Zimándköz, *Zsigmondháza*

Boros-jenõi járás
Székhely: *Boros-Jenõ*
Algyest, *Apatelek, Apáti, Barakony*, Berza, Bokszeg, *Csermõ*, Gurba, Gyarmata, Monyoró, Moroda, Repszeg, Sikula, *Somoskesz, Csigerél-Szõlõs*, Vojvogyén

Pécskai járás
Székhely: *Pécska*
Ó-Bodrog, Forray-Nagy-Iratos, *Magyar-Pécska, Ó-Pécska, Kis-Pereg, Német-Pereg, Szemlak*, Nagy-Varjas, Kis-Varjas

Boros-sebesi járás
Székhely: Boros-sebes
Almás, Baltyele, Berindia, Bogyest, Bohány, Boncesd, Brusztureszk, *Buttyin*, Al-Csill, Dézna, Diécs, Doncsény, Dulcsele, Fényes, Govosdia, Gurahonc, Holdmézes, Honcisor, Ignest, Jószás, Jószáshely, Kakaró, Kertes, Kiszindia, Kocsuba, Krokna, Laáz, Madzirest, Minyád, Monyásza, Musztesd, Nadalbest, Nyágra, Pajsán, Prezest, Ravna, Revetis, Rossia, Bucsava-Solymos, Szaturó, Székács,

Italian Gazetteer

For Italian towns I have found an online search page developed by Daniel E. Niemiec at the following web address: http://www.rootsweb.ancestry.com/~itappcnc/pipcntown.htm. This database contains over 47, 000 place names This is a simple search and for best results use Italian names or drop the ending of the name and check the "starts with" function. Below is a screen print of the search page.

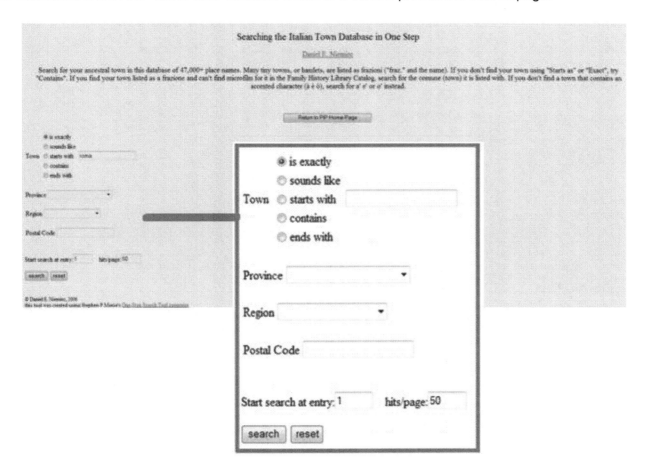

Swedish Gazetteers

Town names are very important in Swedish genealogy research. Many people have similar names and you need the name of the farm or village to determine if an individual is a relative. Another factor to be aware of when you are doing your Swedish research is that each Swedish farms have their own names and some farm names date back to the Viking age or early medieval times. Also note that many areas of Sweden had no villages at all and only the names of individual farms are listed on records.

When reviewing maps and records you need to be familiar with the names of nearby parishes and you should have a list of farms and villages within the parish to make it easier to understand and read the place names written in old handwriting.

In using Swedish gazetteers, remember that similar names were used in different areas of Sweden and more than one place should be checked to find the correct location for your ancestor. Modern spellings may differ from the pre-1906 time period because of the spelling reform of 1906. The spellings of names and places may also be very hard to follow because names may have been written phonetically by clergy and others. Some places may be hard to find and were not included because they are obsolete, very small, or were simply omitted. Using gazetteers and remembering the above factors can help in your genealogical research.

There are a number of Swedish gazetteers available that are useful in identifying town names. Familysearch.org lists the following on their Wiki page:

- **Svensk Ortförteckning**
- **Svenska Orter**
- **Svenska Ortnamn 1999**
- **Ortnamnsregistret**
- **Sveriges församlingar genom tiderna (Swedish Parishes throughout time)**
- **Geografiskt-Statistiskt Handlexikon Öfver Sverige**

Geografiskt-Statistiskt Handlexikon Öfver Sverige was first printed in 1883 and should prove to be the most useful because it describes Sweden at the time when emigration was at its peak and includes all parishes, most villages and larger farms. This gazetteer gives over 65,000 places within Sweden.

This gazetteer is excellent for showing the spellings of Swedish place names prior to the spelling reform which took place in 1906. Some of the main points in the 1906 spelling reform to keep in mind in searching for a place name are:
- f, fv, fw, hv, and hw as signs of the V-sound were replaced by V.
- DT was changed to T or TT
- C was in most places replaced by K and is used today mostly to make a double K, which is written CK.

Helpful vocabulary:
Gård - Farm
By -Village
Socken (Sn) - Parish
Härad (Hd) - District
Län - County

This directory is available at some library, archives, and research institutions as well as in microfilm, fiche, or CD form.
1. Family History Centers: films #873,678 and 873,679 (both necessary for entire set)
2. SVAR and Sveriges Släktforskarförbund have extracted the information into a database and offers it on a CD that is available for purchase at the online bookshop for Sveriges Slaktforskarförbund at this website: http://genealogi.netrix.se/shop/
3. It is also available to subscribers of the SVAR website (see http://www.svar.ra.se/). It is under "Shortcuts – Databases" with the name Rosenberg – Geographic Dictionary of Sweden.

Using Wikipedia in your search

Wikipedia the online encyclopedia has also been helpful for me to find the birthplaces of immigrants. To use Wikipedia, the first few syllables of the name you are searching should be accurate. This will allow you to type in the names you have very slowly and as you start typing in your name, possible selections will show up in the drop down search box. The ending of the name may be wrong but when you type the name in slowly the possible selections will slowly be reduced and you may be able to identify 2-5 possible locations. The Wikipedia pages for your selections will include their GPS coordinates that you can use to locate the town on a map. By finding various selections on maps and matching them to the location of the other names you have, you may be able to group town names in close proximity to one another and determine which location has the strongest possibility of being the birthplace of your ancestor. Remember that the maps you will be using will show modern names and the names may have different endings from the ones that you found in your document searches. Again look for clusters of names that may have spelling variations that are close to each other. The process outlined above is not 100 percent accurate but is a reasonable process to use. Also remember that the only way to verify that you have found the correct location is to find records for your ancestors.

The illustration at the right is the right hand portion of the page from Wikipedia for Oradea that shows the GPS coordinates for the location of the town.

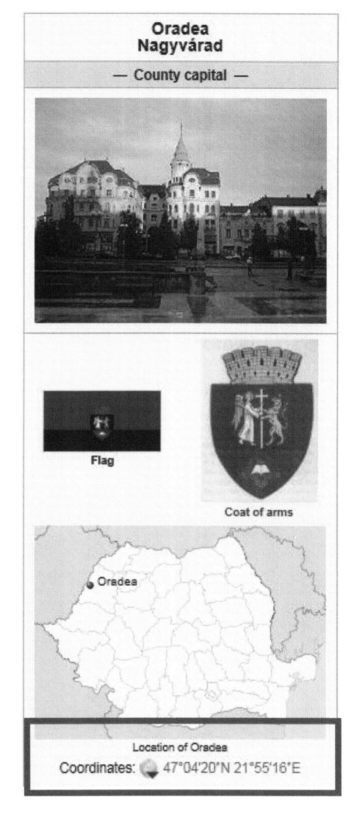

Oradea
Nagyvárad

— County capital —

Flag

Coat of arms

Oradea

Location of Oradea

Coordinates: 47°04'20"N 21°55'16"E

I have found that Wikipedia can also be used as a quick reference in finding villages that had different names based on languages. Below is the Wikipedia page for Oradea that lists its different names in different languages of the different ethnic groups who have lived there.

Note the name of the town in Romanian, Hungarian, German, Turkish, Yiddish and Italian

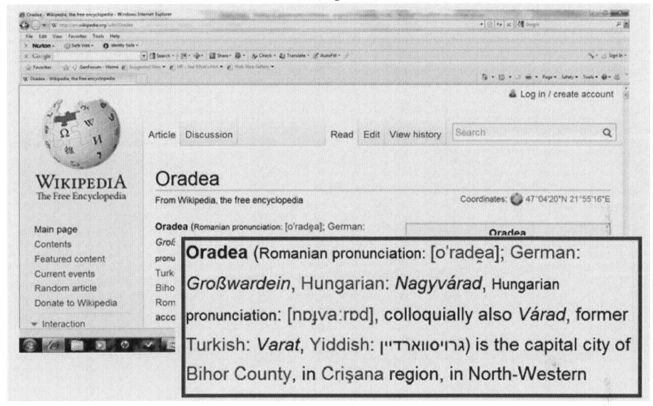

Gazetteers for other countries

The gazetteers that I described above are the gazetteers that I have found online or in libraries. There may be more available for these countries and for other countries and I will continue to search to add to the list. For countries that I did not cover in the Gazetteers listed above, I would suggest using the Wiki pages on Familysearch.org website to see what is available.

Maps

Using maps is very important to locate your ancestor's birthplace. You will need to locate most of your place names in a cluster on a map to identify the most logical location for your ancestor's birthplace. Older maps from the area that your ancestor immigrated should be used because some towns may no longer appear on modern maps.

Older detail maps are available from the National Archives, the Library of Congress, county agencies, and other libraries and historical societies. The University of Wisconsin also has a very good collection of older maps.

I have found that the set of Austrian Military Maps from about 1910 are also very useful. This set of maps cover most of Europe and you can download a map for a specific area clicking on the grid found on the website:

http://lazarus.elte.hu/hun/digkonyv/topo/3felmeres.htm.

Below is the first page at the above website to select one of the 1910 Austrian Military maps.

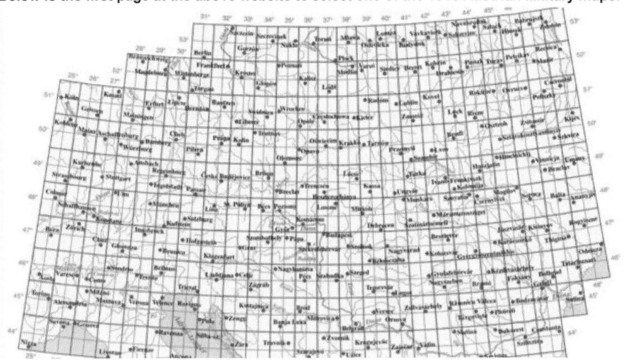

Clicking on one of the grid section will bring up the map below on the right. Please note the detail that it shows. The section outlined in red is a portion of the larger map shown next to it.

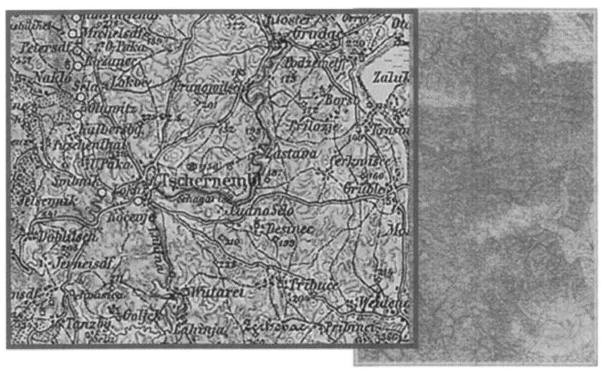

If you have ancestors who immigrated from Galicia, Matthew Bielawa's website www.halgal.com has links to some excellent maps and other information on Galicia.

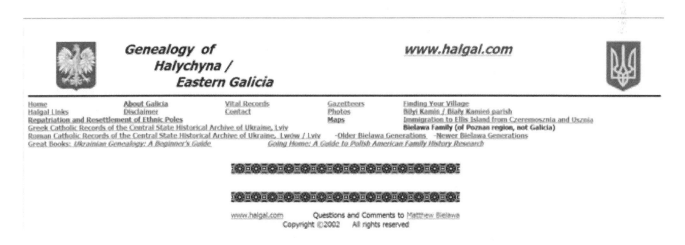

The Map Library on the website of the **Federation of East European Family History Societies** also has a large collection of older European maps. You can view and access these maps at:

http://www.feefhs.org/maplibrary.html

Genealogyunlimited.com also has a great selection of maps. The reprint of the **1817 map of Poland by** N. R. Hewitt is an example of the maps that are available for purchase. This map of Poland was first issued in London in 1817 and shows Poland divided into its internal districts. The map has rich detail, locating cities, small towns and villages.

Final comments on using maps

1. Using multiple maps may be helpful to find the correct location. One map may show some of the names and a map from another source may fill in a few more.

2. Find an area on a map that has as many place names from your list as possible. This is probably the area where your ancestor was born. One of the smaller villages is probably where he was born and a nearby larger town is the location for the parish church where the births, marriages and deaths were recorded.

Step Four - Find records and translate

The next step in our search for our ancestors is to now look for sources of records. The following are a number of resources for European records.

Family Search Centers
(FHC- previously Family History Library)

I have found that the best place to begin this part of your research is to check what is available at http://www.familysearch.org which is the revised website for the Family History Centers. This website gives you access to the 2.4 million rolls of microfilm and over 742,000 microfiche that are stored at the Salt Lake City Genealogical Library. The Salt Lake City Genealogical Library was founded in 1894 to gather genealogical records and assist members of The Church of Jesus Christ of Latter-Day Saints with their family history and genealogical research. It is the largest library of its kind in the world. . A majority of the records contain information about persons who lived before 1930. Approximately 200 cameras are currently microfilming records in over 45 countries. Records have been filmed in over 110 countries, territories, and possessions. In 2003, the collection increased monthly by an average of 4,100 rolls of film, 700 books, and 16 electronic resources.

FHC Online digitized records

Since January 2010, this website has offered the researcher the ability to view digitalized images of their films. Although the number of images available for online viewing has surpassed all other online websites, Familysearch has only touch the surface of the images that they have in their vaults. I have found images for the vital records for the following European countries: Austria, Belgium, Denmark, England, Finland, France, Italy, Liechtenstein, Luxemburg, Netherlands, Norway, Poland, Portugal, Romania, Russia, Slovakia, Spain, Sweden and Switzerland. New databases and images are being added daily so try to find your ancestors in these databases first before ordering films.

If the films have not yet been added to the online databases, you will need to search the catalog to find the film number that you can order and view at their Family History Centers or during a visit to the Salt Lake City Genealogical Library. If you visit Salt Lake City, the library is open to the general public at no charge and it is visited by an estimated 1,900 or more individual patrons each day.

Viewing films at Family History Centers

To view your films at a Family History Center (FHC) please follow the procedure below for a step-by-step procedure to find the find numbers of the records for your ancestors and then how to order and view them.

Before you can order FHC films, you will need to setup your account. FHC films must be ordered online and you must setup a FHC account before you can order. Your account requires you to setup a default FHC where your films will be sent for viewing and your email address for notification of shipment of the films. Payment for the rental of the films can be done with a credit card or through the services of PayPal.com. Films can be ordered for one month or for extended loan.

Your first step will be to find your nearest Family History Center.

Finding Family History Center locations

To find the location of your local family History Center:

      1. Click on "Family Center" in the tool bar on the www.familysearch.org home page.

      2. Next type in your zip code and the next page will show a list of your nearest Family History Centers where you can order and view the films.

Next search the FHC catalog for films to order.

1. To search the online records use the search Box A. To search the library catalog for film numbers select Library Catalog (circle B) on the home page to start your search

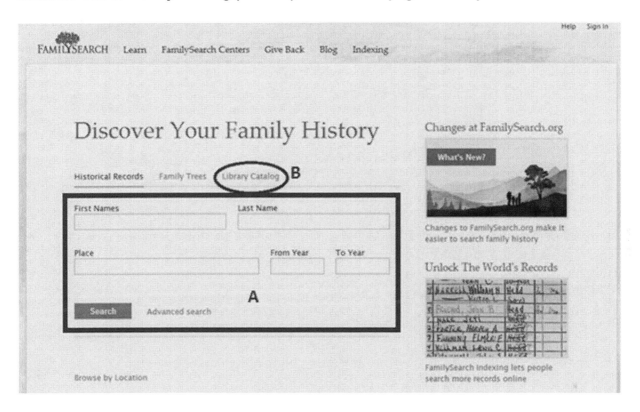

2. Select Place Search on the Library Catalog Page

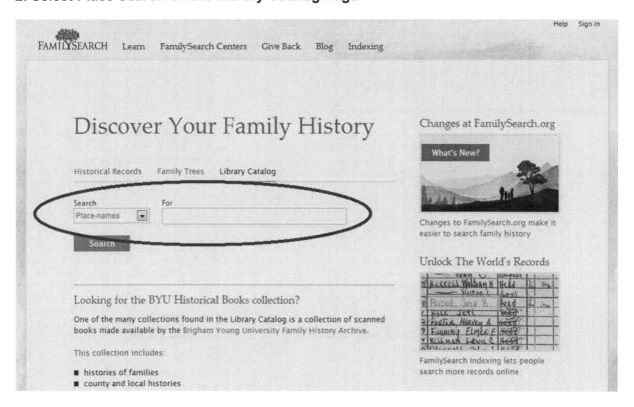

3. Select the files that you want view

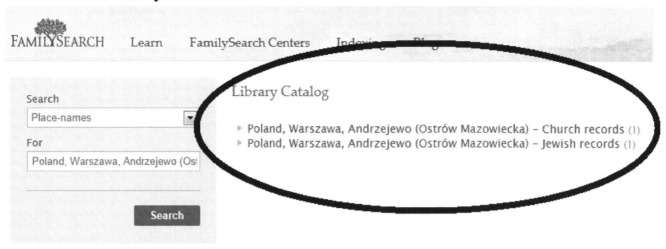

4. Below is a list of films that are available and the film numbers for the location. This page can easily be copied and pasted to a text document to be easily viewed offline later.

Kopie ksiąg metrykalnych, 1808-1881

« Back to search results

authors:	Kościół rzymsko-katolicki. Parafja Andrzejewo (Ostrów Mazowiecka), (Main Author)
format:	Manuscript/On Film
language:	Polish
publications:	Salt Lake City, Utah : Mikrofilmowało The Genealogical Society of Utah, 1969, 1988
physical:	na 10 rolkach mikrofilmu, 35 mm.

Notes

Mikrofilm zrobiony z rękopisów w Archiwum Państwowym, Warszawa i Archiwum Państwowe w Białystoku.

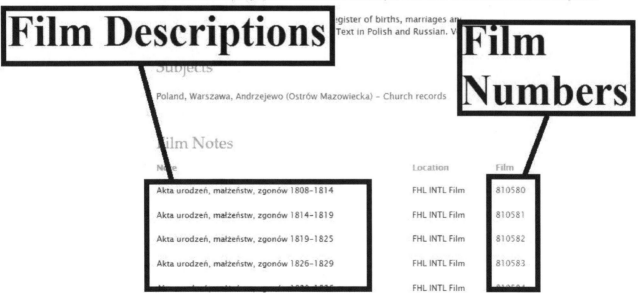

When the films are received by your local FHC, their check in procedure will trigger an email notifying you that the film is ready for viewing at your default FHC. Some locations may also have someone call to inform you that your films are now available for you to review. Each FHC will have viewing machines for you to use to search the films for records that pertain to your ancestors. Many of the records will have indexes at the end of each section to enable you to find your ancestors faster. Check for an index before you start browsing the films image by image. Using the indexes will speedup your research.

Record Format

The vital records that you find will usually be in two formats – narrative or columnar. Below you will find samples of both formats.

Sample record from Family History Center film

Below is a marriage record for Pawel Cmielewski and Balbina. It is a sample of a Polish marriage record that is in the narrative format. I have included a translation below the record.

Narrative format

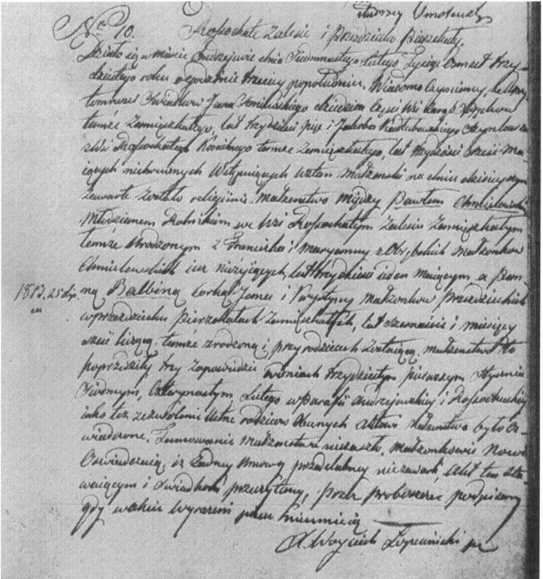

Translation of Marriage record for Pawel Chmielewski and Balbina

This happened in the city of Andrzejewo on <u>the 12th of Feb. in the year 1830</u> at 3 p.m. came in the witnesses Jan Chmielewski 35 yrs old a land owner from the village of ....? and residing there also present was Jakub Kaltubowski a landlord from the village of Pierzchaly - Koscielne and residing there 36 yrs. old and they informed me that today a religious marriage ceremony took place between <u>Pawel Chmielewski</u> a bachelor farmer from the village of Pierzchaly - Zalesie where he was born to the married couple <u>Franciszek and Marianna Obrebska</u> both deceased and between an unmarried woman <u>Balbina</u> sixteen years old the daughter of <u>Jan and Krystyna</u> a married couple the ....? residents of Pierzchaly who was born there and lived there being supported by her parents. This marriage ceremony preceded three marriage banns on the following dates: 31st of January, the 7th & 14th of February of this year in the Parishes of Andrzejewo and also in the village of Pierzchaly - Zalesie . They have received verbal permission to marry and no objections were made to this marriage. The newlyweds informed me that they did not have a pre-nuptial agreement of any kind. This recording was read to the present witnesses by me and it was signed by me only since none of the present witnesses could write.

Signed by   (Father Wojciech Lipiecinski)

Sample Record from Family History Center film

Below is a page from a Polish church's register of deaths. This is a sample of the Columnar format. Note that the headings are in Latin.

Columnar Format

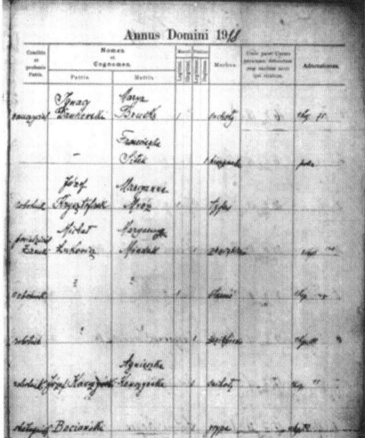

Ancestry.com or Ancestry Library Edition

Ancestry is best known for the U.S. databases that are in its catalog but this website also offers many European databases. Its best offering is the Swedish records it added when it purchased Genline.com. Records for other countries found in these databases are from England, Ireland, Canada, Australia, Russia, Poland, Germany, Czech, France, Italy, Austria, Denmark, Netherlands, Norway and Switzerland. Note that many of these databases are indexes of extracted information and do not offer viewing the original documents. TO find where to look for the original documents, review the description of the database and where the documents are located. Ancestry is a fee based website that offers monthly and annual plans. To access the non-US records requires an upgrade to the World subscription level. Ancestry databases can also be accessed at many local libraries using Ancestry Library Edition which gives access to all databases – US and non-US.

List of Swedish records in Ancestry.com databases

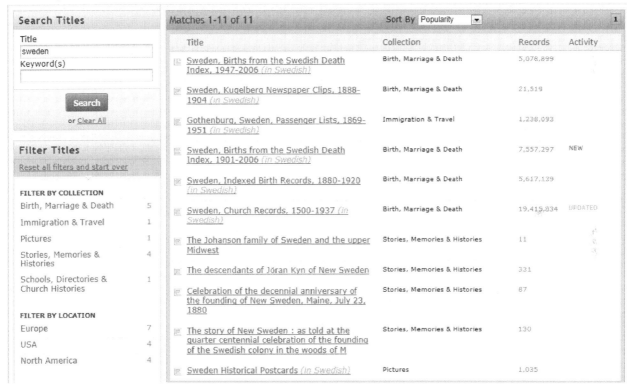

Ancestry.com in other countries - Ancestry.com has affiliates in the countries listed below. Note that these websites are in the language of the country.

United Kingdom - http://www.ancestry.co.uk/

Canada (in English) - http://www.ancestry.ca/

Canada (in French) - http://www.ancestry.ca/?lcid=3084

Australia - http://www.ancestry.com.au/

Germany - http://www.ancestry.de/home/

Italy - Ancestry.it/

France - http://www.ancestry.fr/

Sweden - http://www.ancestry.se/

Sources by country

Germany - summary of record sources

- **Familysearch.org** (online databases and films), **Ancestry.com** and **Ancestry.de** are the main sources of German records that are available online or on film.

- **The Matricula site** at (http://matricula-online.eu/) is another online source and contains some digitized church records from other German and Austrian archives and it also includes inventories (lists) of many Lutheran church records from Eastern areas, including Ostpreussen, Schlesien, Posen, Brandenburg, Pommern and Westpreussen. The Eastern area data was contributed by the Evangelical Central Archive of Berlin (EZAB) but as of January 2010 only the EZAB inventory has been posted, not the digitized images of records.

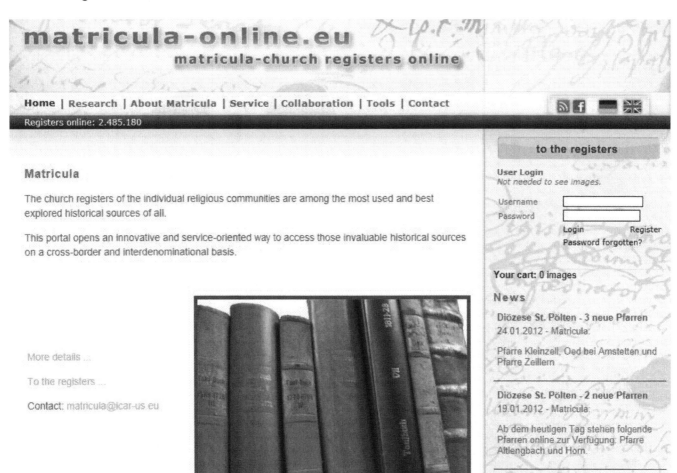

- Another useful website is **Kirchenbuchportal** (church book portal) at http://www.kirchenbuchportal.findbuch.net/php/main.php?ar_id=3708. It was created by the Association of Church Archives to facilitate access to German-language church records. As of July 2010 several archives have posted detailed inventories of the parish registers in their collections. Its pages contain details about the participating archives, including links to posted inventories.

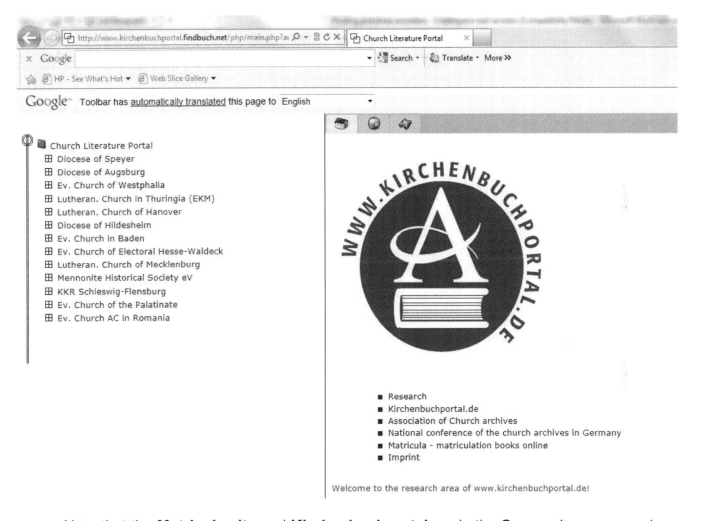

- Note that the **Matricula site** and **Kirchenbuchportal** are in the German language and you must use an online translator to navigate through their pages.

- **2009 change in privacy laws** - Another important event happened on 1 Jan 2009. The German rights-to-privacy laws with regard to to post-1875 civil registration birth, marriage and death certificates have been relaxed. Under the new law, births are available after 110 years, marriages after 80 years and deaths after 30 years, as long as all persons mentioned in the record are dead. The law also provides for older records to be transferred from the local civil registration office to an archive for easier access.

Poland Genealogy Records

Many Polish records can be found on Familysearch.org in their online databases and on their FHC films if not found in the online databases. Other online Polish resources can be found at the websites for the Poznan Marriage project, Geneteka, Polish Roots and the Internet Polish Genealogical Source (iPGS) .

Poznan Marriage Indexing Project - This is a website that I have used to find Polish marriage records. Note that this is an index and only covers records for Poznan Province. Once you have found your ancestors, the website will list the FHC films that are available for the parish where the marriage was performed. Search the database online at:

http://bindweed.man.poznan.pl/posen/project.php

This website has indexed the marriage records from FHC films for the Poznan province from 1820 to 1889. If you are able to find your ancestor in this index, you will find a list of films that you can order to view the digital images of the records. Using this website may be helpful if you cannot find enough data to find your ancestor's birthplace.

Step 1 - The Poznan Marriage Indexing Project Home Page – click of "search the databases"

Step 2 - Search Page - enter names of groom and bride

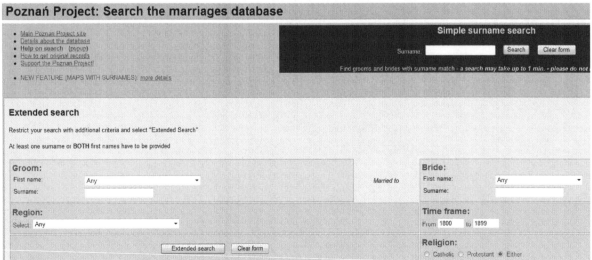

Step 3 - Results Page – click on the town name to see the list of film numbers

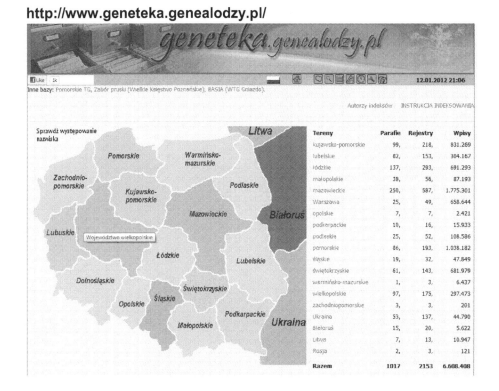

Geneteka - This is a Polish genealogy site that has a searchable database of indexes from church books. The site is in Polish. After selecting a province (e.g. Wielkopolskie or Kujawsko-pomorskie), you can search for names in the records that they have indexed so far. There are a few Protestant records included, e.g. Kreuz parish in Poznan city.

http://www.geneteka.genealodzy.pl/

Polish Roots

The Polish Roots website at www.polishroots.org does not host any databases but lists some websites that have searchable databases and many resources that will be helpful in your research.

The website includes links to databases such as Antwerp Alien Registrations, Bremen Passenger Lists 1920-1939, Immigrants to Canada, Canadian Naturalization 1915-1951, and many more. The website also includes many pages that help the researcher with alphabets, calendars, letter writing, culture, customs, geography, maps, heraldry, tips for the beginning researcher, tips for translating documents, lists of resources by country, ethnic group and region.

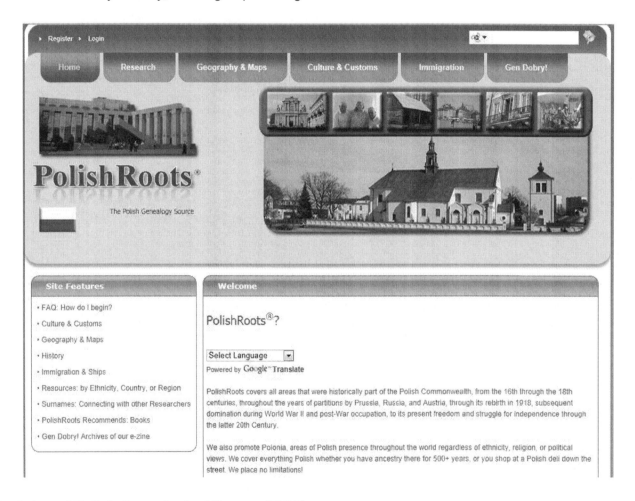

The Internet Polish Genealogical Source (iPGS)

A new resource for Polish research is the website the Internet Polish Genealogical Source (iPGS) at http://www.ipgs.us/. Some of the material you can find at this site includes:

- Dachau German Concentration Camp Records
- Iwona's Research, including information on about 52,000 names and about 2,800 towns
- Roman Catholic Church in Belarus
- Genealogy InTime Magazine
- Genealogy guide to About 130+ Google Search Engines
- Information from and about Iwona Dakiniewicz
- 1907 Atlas (Kingdom of Poland Maps)
- Herbarz Polski (Surname Heraldic Descriptions)
- Articles by Iwona Dakiniewicz (Polish Genealogical Information)
- Parish Histories (Histories of US Parishes)

The 1907 Atlas has very detailed maps. You will also find a nice table of countries, often associated with Polish research, that contain links within each country to archives, cemetery records, family websites, heraldry, newspapers, researchers, surnames and a whole lot more.

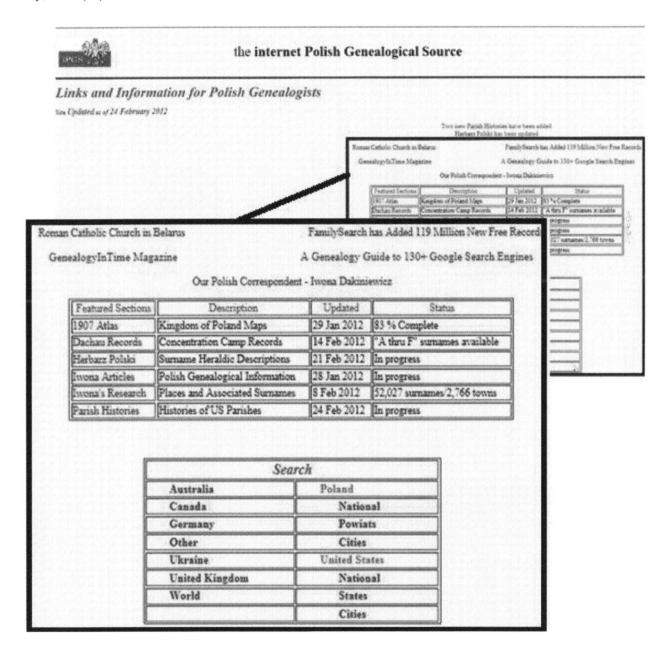

Hungarian research

A few Hungary databases can be found in the online listings for Familysearch.org and Ancestry.com. The FHC catalog also has many films that will contain images church records.

Another website that has more online Hungarian databases is the Hungary Exchange. This website tries to help researchers who need assistance with their Hungarian genealogy and Hungarian research. It includes many databases that are not listed on other websites and many have been contributed by Hungarian researchers. The goal of the website is sharing information and working together. Researchers can tackle genealogical obstacles, brick-walls and find more information for Hungarian family trees. There is a link on the website to share or contribute records and documents.

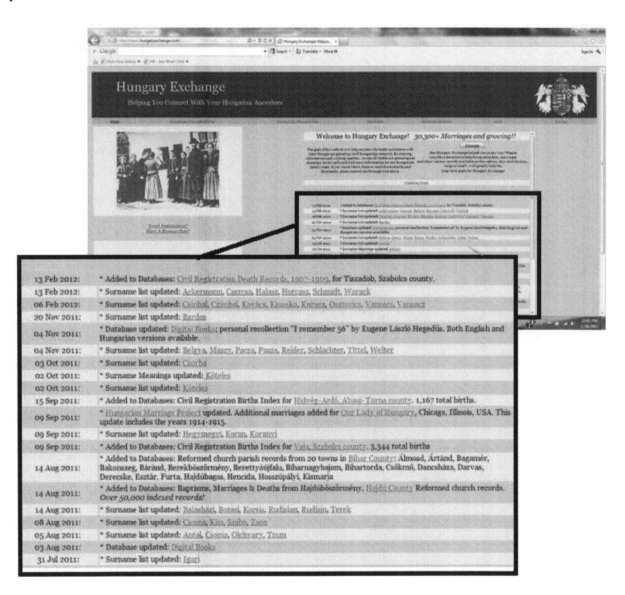

Czech Republic Genealogy Records

The Familysearch.org Wiki page for the Czech Republic lists the websites for the country's regional archives that are in the process of uploading digital images of their church registers for births, marriages and deaths. To access these images you must register but access is free. From the Wiki page you can click on the location of the archive and you will go to their websites where you will be able to search records for your ancestors. Each archive is doing this on separate schedules and some like Trebon are almost complete. If you cannot find your ancestors, please be patient because the archives are adding images daily. The archive at Trebon was the first to put their records online and the others are slowly doing the same. Below is the web address for Familysearch.org's Wiki page for the Czech Republic.

https://www.familysearch.org/learn/wiki/en/Czech_Republic_Archives_and_Libraries

Familysearch.org's Wiki page for the Czech Republic

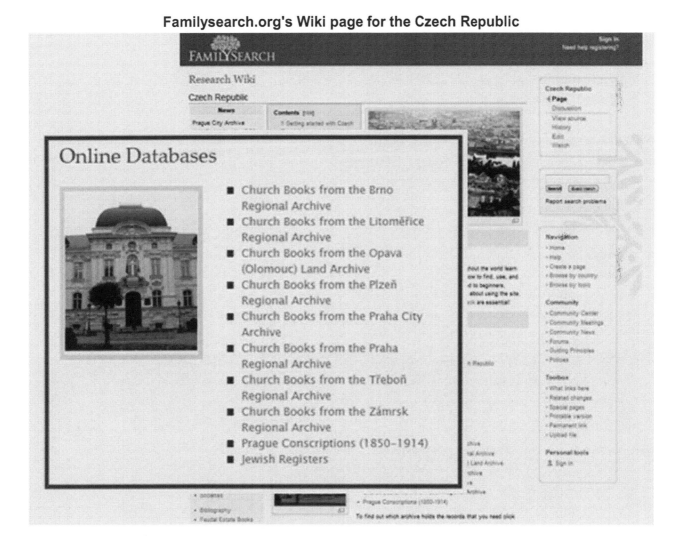

Below are samples of the Trebon pages and a sample of the records that can be found.

Below is the main page for the Czech Digital Archives at Trebon at:

http://digi.ceskearchivy.cz/index_main.php?doctree=1n&lang=en

1. To find your ancestral village, click "Geographical Index"

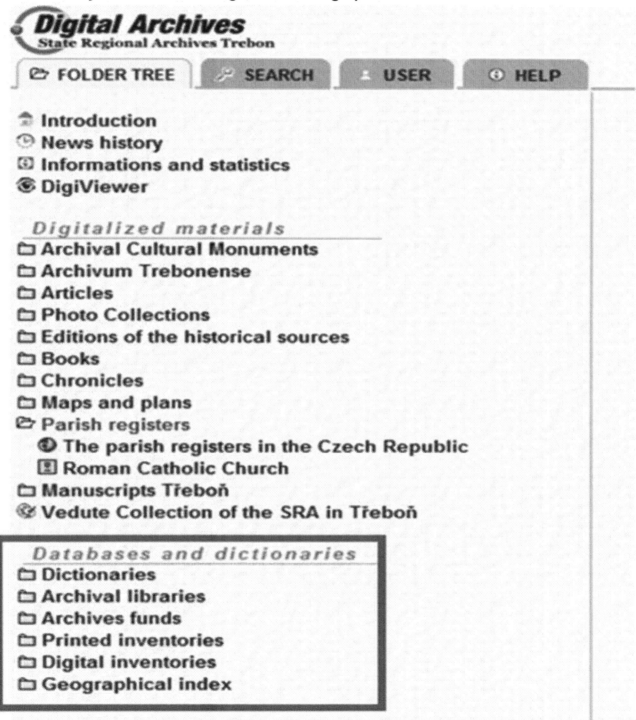

2. This will take you to a page where you need to select the first letter of the village and next you will be at a page where all of the villages for that letter will be listed in the left column and the parishes will be listed in the right column. When you find the village, click on the parish.

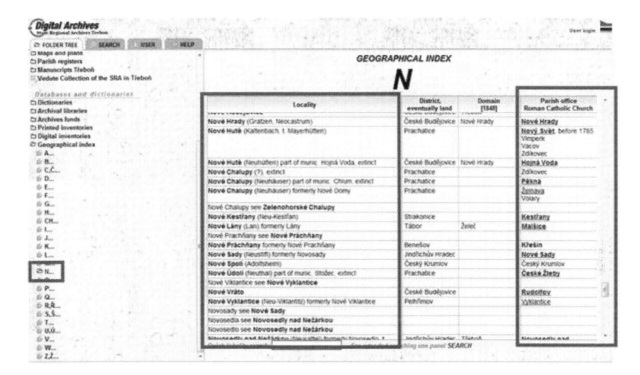

3. Next you will be at a page that will list all of the registers (books) that are available to search. Click on the register that includes the record type (birth, marriage, death) and the year range that you want to search.

	Type	Time extent	Records of	Time extent by type	Note
Book 1	BMD	1630-1679	whole parish district	B 1630-1679 M 1631-1679 D 1631-1679	
Book 2	BMD	1677-1715	whole parish district	B 1677-1715 M 1678-1715 D 1678-1715	
Book 3	BMD	1715-1766	whole parish district	B 1715-1766 M 1715-1766 D 1715-1766	
Book 4	BMD	1767-1784	whole parish district	B 1767-1784 M 1767-1784 D 1767-1784	
Book 5	BMD	1784-1818	Nové Hrady	B 1784-1812 M 1784-1807 D 1784-1818	
Book 6	B	1812-1842	Nové Hrady		
Book 7	B	1842-1854	Nové Hrady		
Book 8	M	1807-1856	Nové Hrady		
Book 9	D	1819-1852	Nové Hrady		
Book 10	M	1854-1856	whole parish district		
Book 11	M	1919-1923	whole parish district		
Book 12	BM	1854-1865	Nové Hrady	B 1854-1862 M 1856-1865	
Book 13	BM	1862-1881	Nové Hrady	B 1862-1872 M 1865-1881	
Book 14	M	1881-1919	Nové Hrady		
Book 15	B	1872-1906	Nové Hrady		
Book 16	D	1852-1889	Nové Hrady		
Book 17	D	1890-1922	Nové Hrady		
Book 18	BMD	1784-1864	Byňov, Jiříkovo Údolí	B 1784-1843 M 1788-1856 D 1784-1864	
Book 19	BMD	1843-1892	Byňov	B 1843-1892 M 1857-1891 D 1865-1891	
Book 20	BMD	1821-1886	Jiříkovo Údolí	B 1821-1882	

Sample Czech records

Irish Genealogy Records

Below is a list of websites that offer help or searchable databases of Irish records.

1. Find My Past – Ireland - http://www.findmypast.ie/ (offers searchable database of Irish records)

2. Irish Genealogy - http://www.irishgenealogy.ie/ (searchable database of some Irish records that displays extracted information)

3. The Irish Genealogical Society (IGSI) - http://www.irishgenealogical.org/ (offers helpful information on Irish genealogy)

Findmypast.ie was launched in May 2011 to help find Irish genealogy records. It is a joint venture between Findmypast.co.uk and Engelmann, the award-winning Irish history and Heritage Company. Findmypast.ie will host the most extensive collection of Irish land records available anywhere online and will be a valuable resource for those 80 million people worldwide who claim Irish ancestry.

Findmypast.ie, which is aimed at those of Irish descent including 13 per cent of the US population, carries the most detailed and thorough collection of Irish records ever seen in one place – over 4 million records. These include land records, directories, wills, obituaries, gravestone inscriptions and marriages.

The earliest records date back to the 13th century (wills) and include several important collections from the 18th century (The Elphin Census 1749 and the 1798 Rebellion records). The collection includes the exclusive publication of the Landed Estates Court records, a crucial resource for the mid- to late-19th century, which includes details of over 500,000 tenants on Irish estates.

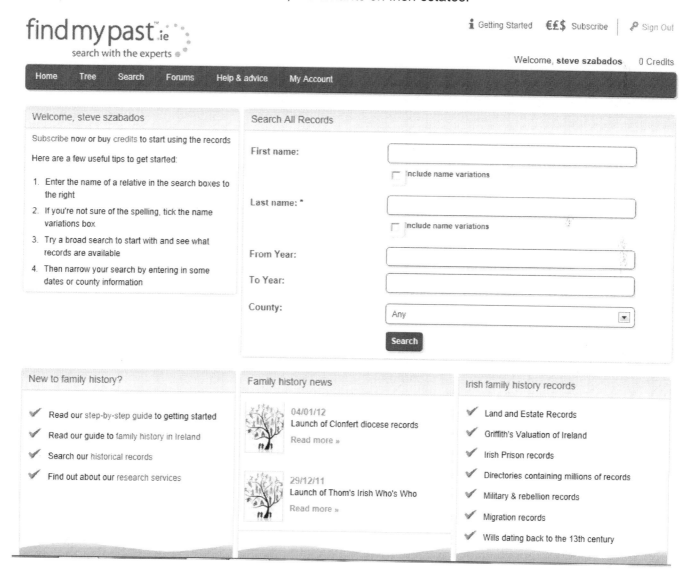

Findmypast.ie offers documents that include - land/estates, Courts/legal, Military/rebellion, Census, Travel/migration, vital records (BMD), and Directories

FindmyPast.ie - results summary

findmypast™.ie
search with the experts

ℹ Getting Started   €£$ Subscribe   🔑 Sign Out

Welcome, **steve szabados**   0 Credits

| Home | Tree | Search | Forums | Help & advice | My Account |

Home > Search Results

Refine your search

First name: james

☐ Include name variations

Last name: * mcdonough

☐ Include name variations

From Year:

To Year:

County: Any ▾

Search

Results

Land and estates	34	View
Courts and legal	57	View
Military and rebellion	1	View
Census and substitutes	0	
Travel and migration	0	
Vital records (BMDs)	5	View
Directories	1	View

FindmyPast.ie - results (click "More details" to see documents)

findmypast™.ie
search with the experts

ℹ Getting Started   €£$ Subscribe   🔑 Sign Out

Welcome, **steve szabados**   0 Credits

| Home | Tree | Search | Forums | Help & advice | My Account |

Home > Search Results > Vital-records-(BMDs) > Deaths and Burials

Search

First name: james

☐ Include name variations

Last name: * mcdonough

☐ Include name variations

From Year:

To Year:

County: Any ▾

Search

Total records 4 for Deaths and Burials in Vital records (BMDs)

First name	Last name	County	Source	View
James	McDonough	Cork	Tipperary Clans Archive	More Details
James	McDonough		Tipperary Clans Archive	More Details
James	McDonough	Galway	Tipperary Clans Archive	More Details
James	McDonough	Tipperary	Tipperary Clans Archive	More Details

If you do not have a subscription, you will see this page as you try to view specific documents documents. Findmypast.ie offers 6 month and 12 month subscriptions and a PayAsYouGo option at reasonable fees.

FindmyPast.ie - results

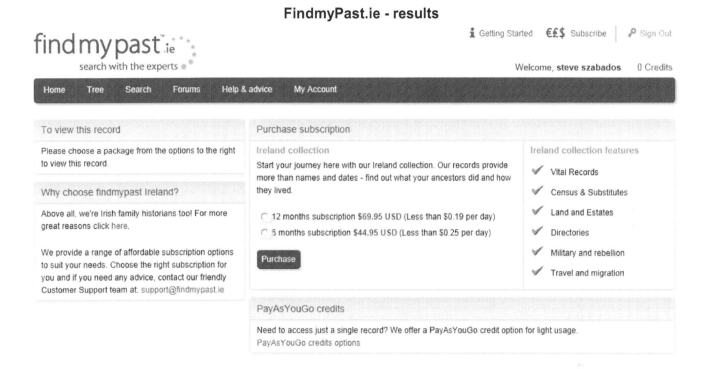

England & Scotland genealogy sources

- Find My Past UK - www.findmypast.co.uk

  FindMyPast.co.uk is a UK dedicated site that gives users the opportunity to research their family history and construct their family tree using a vast quantity of online records. With more than 170 million names in family trees and with more than 250,000 new records added each week, this site certainly has a lot to offer. The site focuses entirely upon UK and Scottish users. This is a fee based website that offers six month and 12 month subscriptions plus a pay per record option.

  Membership of FindMyPast.co.uk allows users to search through census records and trace births, marriages and deaths, in order to discover their family history and generate their family tree. FindMyPast.co.uk has more than 23 million parish records listing baptisms, marriages and burials to get you truly immersed in local records making your search more exciting. Furthermore, FindMyPast.co.uk allows users to follow a step-by-step guide to growing and expanding their family tree. Users can upload an existing GEDCOM file, or use powerful family tree builder software to create a family tree from scratch.

  Excellent privacy settings allow users to share their research with friends, family and loved ones (by applying a password to their research) or share it with the world by making the research public.

Findmypast.co.uk Home Page

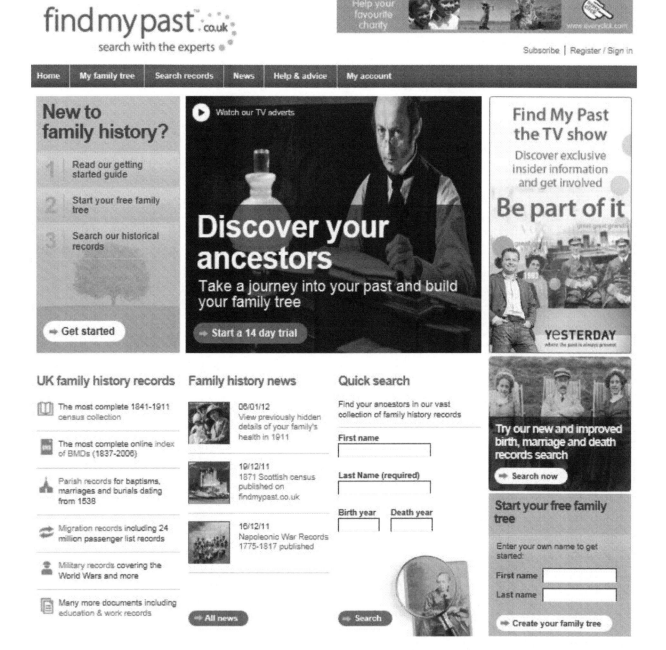

Enter the name you are search and their birth and death dates if known to see possible documents on the results summary page.

Findmypast.co.uk offers documents that include - Census/land/survey, Births, Marriages, Deaths, Church/religion, Military/war, Travel/migration, Institutions/organizations, Education/work and directories.

Findmypast.co.uk Results Summary Page

Subscribe | Register / Sign in

| Home | My family tree | Search records | News | Help & advice | My account |

Family history records on findmypast.co.uk

Record collections

 refine current search

 start a new search

Census, land and surveys 14,019 results	Number of results
1841 Census	➡ 1,290 records
1851 Census	➡ 1,340 records
1861 Census	➡ 1,391 records
1871 Census	➡ 1,653 records
1881 Census	➡ 1,682 records
1891 Census	➡ 1,679 records

Findmypast.co.uk results page

Getting started Subscribe Register / Sign In

| Home | My family tree | Search records | News | Help & advice | My account |

Parish Records Collection - baptism search results

Search criteria used:

First name(s): **John**
Last name: **Howard**

Results:
1045 records found.

Cost:
PayAsYouGo customers who do not have a subscription will be charged to view these records. The cost in credits varies according to the amount of detail in the records, and the record source. If you do not have a subscription for these records, subscribe now for unlimited access.

Visit our Knowledge Base to find out what parish records we offer.

⬅ all search results

redefine search

Viewing Page 1 of 21 [1] 2 3 4 5 6 7 8 9 10 >>

Last name	First name(s)	Year of baptism	Place	County	Details	Image
BROADBENT-HOWARD	John Charles	1855	Mottram-In-Longdendale	Cheshire	VIEW	VIEW
CLEMENCE HOWARD	John Thomas	1876	Runcorn	Cheshire	VIEW	VIEW
CROMPTON OR HOWARD	John	1751	Royton	Lancashire	VIEW	VIEW
HEYWOOD ALIAS HOWARD	John	1820		Devon	VIEW	N/A
HOWARD	John	1563	Bungay	Suffolk	VIEW	N/A
HOWARD	John	1621	Mottram-In-Longdendale	Cheshire	VIEW	VIEW
HOWARD	John	1627	Cambridge, St Botolph	Cambridgeshire	VIEW	N/A

To view the details of of a record you must be registered and to view and download image you must have a subscription or have credits in you PayAsYouGo account.

Subscription info for Findmypast.co.uk as of January 2012

- Scotland's People – www.scotlandspeople.gov.uk
  ScotlandsPeople is the largest online source for original Scottish genealogical information. It has almost 80 million records to search. This fee based website has a comprehensive offering of Scottish census records, Scottish wills, birth certificates and death certificates. They offer a free name search. However, they require you to register and then buy "Purchase vouchers" to view and download a copy of the document.

Scotlandspeople.gov.uk Home Page

Scotlandspeople.gov.uk Results Page

Free and fast starter search results

You searched for "" **"howard"** 1513 - 2009

Refine search

Statutory Registers
Births
Marriages
Deaths

Old Parish Registers
Births & Baptisms
Banns & Marriages
Deaths & Burials

Catholic Registers
Births & Baptisms
Banns & Marriages
Deaths & Burials
Other Events

Census Records
1841 1851 1861 1871 1881
1891 1901 1911 1881 (LDS)

Free Search Records
Wills & Testaments
Coats of Arms

Search results	Found
Census 1841.Learn more.	102 matches
Census 1851.Learn more.	149 matches
Census 1861.Learn more.	230 matches
Census 1871.Learn more.	234 matches
Census 1881.Learn more.	306 matches
Census 1891.Learn more.	306 matches
Census 1901.Learn more.	396 matches
Census 1911.Learn more.	454 matches
Census 1881 (LDS).Learn more.	304 matches
Statutory Register Births 1855 - 2009.Learn more.	2228 matches
Statutory Register Marriages 1855 - 2009.Learn more.	1256 matches
Statutory Register Deaths 1855 - 2009.Learn more.	1584 matches
Old Parish Records Births & Christenings 1538 - 1854.Learn more.	93 matches
Old Parish Records Banns & Marriages 1538 - 1854.Learn more.	127 matches
Old Parish Records Deaths & Burials 1538 - 1854.Learn more.	69 matches
Catholic Parish Records Births & Baptisms 1703 - 1992.Learn more.	164 matches
Catholic Parish Records Marriages 1736 - 1934.Learn more.	13 matches
Catholic Parish Records Deaths & Burials 1742 - 1955.Learn more.	48 matches
Catholic Parish Records Other 1742 - 1909.Learn more.	20 matches
Wills & Testaments 1513 - 1901.Learn more.	28 matches
Arms & Heraldry 1672 - 1908.Learn more.	No exact matches

More UK and Scotland useful sources of information

- Genuki – www.genuki.org.uk
  Genuki is a large collection of informational pages on genealogy for England, Scotland, Wales and Ireland. This is an excellent starting point for genealogy research for these countries.

- National Archives of Scotland – www.nas.gov.uk
  Based in Edinburgh, the National Archives of Scotland (NAS) are the national archives of Scotland. The NAS claims to have one of the most varied collections of archives in Europe. It is the main archive for sources of the history of Scotland as an independent state, her role in the British Isles and the links between Scotland and many other countries over the centuries. In conjunction with the General Register Office for Scotland (GROS), the NAS supplies content for the ScotlandsPeople website, allowing searches in pre-1855 old parish registers (OPRs); statutory registers of births, marriages and deaths from 1855; census returns, 1841-1901; and the testaments digitally captured by the SCAN project

  The NAS has expanded its digitization program begun under the SCAN project. It is currently involved in digitizing the register of sasines (Scotland's property register) and the records of ecclesiastical courts (kirk sessions, presbyteries, synods and the General Assembly of the Church of Scotland). The church court records extend to some five million pages of information and the NAS is, at the time of writing (2008), developing an online access system for large-scale, un-indexed historical sources, in parallel to free access in the NAS's public search rooms, known as "virtual volumes".

- The National Archives of UK – www.nationalarchives.gov.uk
  The National Archives (TNA) is a UK government department and an executive agency of the Secretary of State for Justice. It is "the UK government's official archive, containing 1,000 years of history". There are separate national archives in some of the other parts of the United Kingdom - the National Archives of Scotland holds government and private documents relating to Scotland and the Public Record Office of Northern Ireland holds records for Northern Ireland. Some of the most popular documents have now been digitized and are available to download, via the DocumentsOnline delivery system, for a small fee. All of the open census records have been digitized, and there are also significant other sources online (such as wills proved in the Prerogative Court of Canterbury, 1383-1858).

Jewish Research Summary

Jewish genealogy research for European records spans a number of countries. In 1900, a small population of Sephardic Jews was found in western Germany and in the Netherlands. A much larger population of Ashkenazi Jews were found in eastern Germany, Poland, western Russia and Bohemia, Moravia, Slovakia, Lower Austria, Hungary and Romania.

Research for Jewish genealogical records in European is very similar to research of other ethnic groups. In the 1700 and 1800s, Jewish Rabbis were charged with recording the vital records of their congregations similar to the other religous officials in Europe. In the 1890s, governments began requiring civil registrations for vital records and government archives began saving copies of civil and church records. The chaos of World War II that destroyed many synagogues did not destroy the records in most archives.

There are however unique challenges to Jewish European genealogy research in Eastern Europe.

One challenge was the reluctance of the Ashkenazi Jews to accept surnames. Permanent family surnames exist today but was only accepted by the Jews after it was mandated by the rulers where they were living. The Sephardic Jews accepted durnames as early as the 10th or 11th century. However this practice was not adopted by the Ashkenazi Jews of Germany or Eastern Europe until the 18th and 19th century.

Most Ashkenazi Jews in Europe used the traditional system of patrimonial Hebrew surnames. In the Jewish patronymic system, the first name is followed by either **ben-** or **bat-** ("son of" and "daughter of," respectively), and then the father's name. Exceptions included Jewish communities in large cities such as Prague or Frankfurt, where many of the names were derived from house-signs and rabbinical dynasties, which often used a town name, typically the birthplace of the founder of the dynasty. Such surnames were much easier to shed or change than they would be today, and did not have the official status that modern ones do.

The process of assigning permanent surnames to Ashkenazi Jewish families began in Austria-Hungary. On 23 July 1787, the Austrian emperor Joseph II issued a decree called *Das Patent über die Judennamen* which compelled the Jews to adopt German surnames. Prussia also mandated surnames soon after Emperor Joseph issued his decree. In 1812, after Napoleon had occupied much of Prussia and surname adoption was mandated for the unoccupied parts. Jews in the rest of Prussia adopted surnames in 1845.

At the end of the 18th century after the Partition of Poland, the Russian Ysar found out the he had acquired a large number of Jews who did not use surnames. He then were required they had to adopt surnames during the early 19th century.

During the early 1800s, Jewish families who had not adopted a permanent surname were given one by civil officials. This created problems with genealogical research when the married son living on his own with his wife and children was given a surname different from his parents and brothers. Note that this forced naming was done in the first half of the 1800s and would complicate your research for the second and third generation of European records that you would try to find.

Another challenge when researching Jewish European records was caused by the residency restrictions that were placed on Jews in some countries. After the Jews were forced to leave Palestine, they were never fully accepted in the lands that they lived. Due to various reasons, they were forced to move many times throughout history until most lived in Eastern Europe. The Jews were allowed to live in various areas only if the local nobles gave their approval. The permisson of the nobles were usually depedant on the skills of the Jewish merchants or craftsmen. The ownership of land by the Jews was not permitted. The success of the Jews at these occupations sometimes put them in conflict with the local non-Jews who pressured the local noble to retract his approval of the Jews living in his district. This may have caused Jewish merchants and craftsmen to move multiple times during their lifetime while seeking work. This would make looking for their records and the records for their children and ancestors in one place very difficult.

My great-great grandfather Lazar Frank was born in Ker, Abaúj-Torna County, Hungary about 1838. He married Leni Hartman in about 1864 in Bőcs, Borsod County, Hungary. Their first two children were born in Bőcs, Borsod County, Hungary before they moved to Gesztely, Zemplen County, Hungary in 1869. Two more children were born in Geszlety. By 1900, Leni had died and Lazar was living in Mezocsat, Borsod County, Hungary. I have been able to find four records for the family - the 1900 marriage record for his son Mozes, the 1870 birth record for Mozes, the 1872 birth record for daughter Sara and the 1869 Hungarian census record listing Lazar, Leni and their first two children.

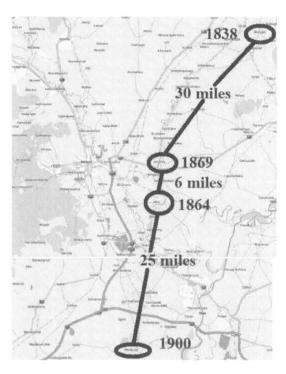

- Could the lack of a surname be preventing me from finding the birth records for Lazar and Leni?
- Could the movement of Lazar with his family be preventing from finding marriage records for his three other children and the death records for him and Leni?

Ancestry.com and Jewishgen.com have indexed many of the FHC films that cover the early rabbinic vital records. Indexed records allow you to find the film image for your ancestor easier. Use the Ancestry.com or Jewishgen.com databases to find the indexed record which then lists the film number. Then use familysearch.org to order the correct film that will allow you to have a copy of the actual record. Remember that the actual record will give you more information than the index. Familysearch.org also is adding the civil records of the late 1890s and early 1900s that they recently were allowed to film.

Holocaust records
Another important aspect of your Jewish family history is the affect of the Holocaust on the family. Your ancestors may have emigrated from Europe before the Holocaust but they may have left relatives that were caught its tragic effects. It is important to find and list the names of the members of your family who were victims or survivors. Jewishgen.com has many lists of the Jews that were transported to the consecration camps. There are also websites for some of the camps where records are being indexed and are searchable by name. Another source is the International Tracing Service. This organization was

founded in 1946 and operated since 1955 by the International Red Cross. The aim of the ITS is to collect information on those who were missing, deported, or incarcerated in concentration camps.

Sources for other countries
Use Familysearch.org Wiki pages to find genealogy sources for all other countries

How to go beyond the beginning date of the last film to add more generations.
Using marriage and death records can add two to three more generations to your family tree. Generally these records will list the ages of the bride and groom or the person who died with their ages. The records will also usually list their parents. Below is an illustrative example of my grandmother's ancestors where I added two generations by reviewing death records:
- Birth Records for my grandmother's village go back to 1808
- Her great-grandmother Balbina Przezdziecki's 1831 birth record listed that her father was Jan Przezdziecki and he was age 36 (born in 1777)
- Jan's 1833 death record listed that his parents were Bartlomiej Przezdziecki & Rozalie Listisnicki (1 additional generation)
- The death record for Rozalie listed that she died in 1831 at age 72 (born 1759) and her parents were Michala Listisnicki (estimated age 25 and born 1734) and Agnes Przezdziecki (estimated age 25 and born in 1734) (2nd additional generation)

Location and Types of records available in the "old country"

Vital records - birth, marriage and death records
Birth, marriage and death records were initially kept by the churches. In the late 1800s civil governments began requiring these events be reported to a civil registrar office in the county. Church officials also continued to record these events. Therefore early vital records are saved in church archives (such as Diocesan archives for Catholic records) and births, marriages and deaths from the the late 1800s and later are stored in both Church archives and the National or Regional archives for each country.

As stated earlier, Family History Centers (FHC) have filmed many early vital records and these early records are available on films that can be rented for viewing at Family History Centers or possibly online at Familysearch.org. Officials did not allow FHC to film all the records stored in their archives and they placed limitations on the age of the films that could be filmed. For example, I believed that Polish church and civil officials only allowed films that were 100 years or older to be filmed. I found that the films for my grandfather's parish stopped at 1885 and films for my grandmother's village stopped at 1870. These examples show that there is a gap of records from the late 1800s that are available for viewing only at the archive. FHC has continued to revisit countries to film later records that now fall within the age restrictions. As these new films are developed and cataloged more records that are needed for the genealogy research of immigrants from the 1800s and early 1900s will be available for viewing at FHC or online at Familysearch.org.

The vital records for some countries such as the Czech Republic, Sweden and the United Kingdom are available online on other websites as discussed earlier in this book. Records for these databases are still governed by the age restrictions, but are usually more current than FHC films because the websites were developed more recently.

If records that you need are not available in FHC films or an online database, you may need to contact the appropriate archive or hire a local researcher to obtain the needed document.

I needed the 1900 Romania marriage record for my great-grandparents to knock down a brick wall. I was able to find and hire a genealogy researcher in Romania who found the marriage record. Below is his email to me that gives me a translation of the records. He also mailed me copies of the original document. The marriage record confirmed that my great-grandfather changed his name and with the correct surname I was able to extend my family tree with two more generations.

Email from Romanian researcher

Dear Mr. Szabados,

I managed to obtain the requested marriage record in the State Archives from Arad. It is preserved in the Fond No. 1250, Register No. 53 and its content in English is the following:

Register of marriages, position No. 6
Issued in Pîncota on February 4, 1900. In front of the Registrar Karoly Kotro appeared as groom Marton Szabados, Roman Catholic, street musician, resident in Pîncota house No. 169, born in Gesztely, Zemplen county on June 15, 1870, son of Lazar Frank, taylor, resident in Mezocsat, Borsod county, and of the deceased wife of Lazar Frank, born Leni Hoffmann, willing to marry Jozefa Szrna, Roman Catholic, street musician, resid. in Pîncota No. 169, born in Opatin on March 19, 1879, daughter of the deceased Janos Szrna, street musician from Pîncota, and the widow of Janos Szrna born Zsuzsanna Trullik, street musician from Pîncota.. Witnesses: Karoly Hradszky, street musician, resid. in Pîncota No. 165, 31 years old; Pal Kulonek, street musician, resid. in PÎNCOTA No. 157, 29 years old. The parts declared that they are willing to marry and the Registrar declared them married. The bride cannot write.

I will send the copy of the record by air-mail on your address.

The charges of this research are as follows:

Travel Cluj-Arad-Cluj			60 Usd
Accomodation			60 Usd
1 record	x	30 Usd	30 Usd
		Total	150 Usd

I would be grateful to have the payment sent by Western Union on my name and address: Ladislau Gheorghe XXXXXXXX (please use all three names as they appear in my ID), Str. Tarnita 1, ap. 28, 400659 Cluj-.Napoca, Romania. Tel. 0040-264-XXXXX.

After sending please communicate by Email or regular air-mail, Fax (0040-264-590251) the Control number of the sending, the exact name of the sender and the amount sent.

Looking forward to your kind confirmation of receipt of this research report, I remain with the best wishes

Ladislau

Other Church records that should be available for genealogists in Diocesan and local parish archives are:

- **Lists of donors' names and lists or census of parishioners** - pastors kept records to insure parishioners that could supported the church.
- **Notes taken by priests** were usually about specific parishioners - this information may have good or bad comments. Church officials may not allow these documents to be viewed because of the possible harmful nature of their contents.
- **Lists of who received First Communion, Confirmation and Anointing of the Sick** plus marriage banns, conscripts and converts.
- **Divorce proceedings** - affidavits for these proceedings may give information of their lives that would not be in other documents.
- **Visitation books** – The books include descriptions of the financial status of the church with the names of the owners, the number of Catholics and non-Catholics, existing schools, hospitals and other major facilities in the parish.

Other Records found in the State Archives and local registry offices that concern genealogists include:

- **Passport applications** - some countries such as Austria and Germany require their citizens to obtain permission if they wanted to immigrate to another country. The application process included documents such as birth records, proof that the emigrant did not owe money, proof that his military service was completed and a waiver of his right to live in the town.
- **Lists of taxpayers** - these were lists of property owners such as land and livestock. This would not be a complete substitute for a census record but would be of interest to the genealogist to know what assets their ancestors owned.
- **Notary records** which included land transactions, loans and financial agreements.
- **Wills or testaments** of relatives who did not emigrate occasionally mention their relatives in foreign lands.
- **Legal proceedings** - ancestors could be included as the defendant, the plaintiff, a witness or a member of the jury. This would be a very important source of information if your ancestor was the defendant or plaintiff in a lawsuit.
- **Land records** for the manor estates - ancestors may not own the manor estate but may be listed as workers on the estate, their wife and children may also be listed.
- **School lists** - this would include list of children and the faculty.
- **Police records** - Police in some countries kept records of each person's residence in the 1800s. Citizens were required to tell the police when they moved. These records could be used as a substitute census record by the genealogist.
- **Hospital records - These** registers usually include the patient's name, sex, age, marital condition, residence, occupation, and religion.
- **Military records** which include lists of conscripts and reservists - Military records of Europe include a number of valuable genealogical sources. The military played a significant role in the lives of citizens of most countries. Prior to 1800 a soldier's term of service in many countries was for life, although he was not necessarily on active duty the entire time. In the 1800s, the term of military service was reduced to a specific number of years - such as 10 years in some countries. Those exempt from military service were the clergy, the nobility, certain government officials, and workers employed in mining, iron production, and necessary agricultural occupations. One facet of Austrian military life that was unusual for the time period was the absence of segregation and discrimination against non-conformist religious groups. Protestants, Catholics, Orthodox, and Jews all served alongside of one another. Soldiers from each group had all of the rights of military membership and all groups held high positions in the Austrian military.

Obtaining records from sources in the "old country"

- Review the websites of the National, Regional or Church Archives to confirm they may have the records or documents that you need. Your request should be for specific documents. Please do not ask for a generic search.
- Also check the websites to see how they require payment.
- Be prepared to send your email or written request in the language of the country – most ethnic genealogy societies offer form letters that can be used for these requests. This is a sign of respect and may generate a more positive response from the archive.
- Hiring a professional researcher may produce better results but this will be more expensive option. However, this may be needed to jump over some brick walls. If you are contemplating hiring a professional researcher, use the guide at wiki.familysearch.org/en/Hiring_a_Professional_Researcher.
  - Deal only with people that are recommended
  - Be careful with payments

One source to help find a professional genealogist is the association of Professional Genealogists. Their website is at http://www.apgen.org/. I used this website to find the researcher in Romania that was able to obtain a critical document for me. Some of the genealogy societies also list recommended researchers in foreign countries. The Polish Genealogy Society of America (PGSA) is one example of this and you can find their list of recommended researchers in their directory at their website (PGSA.org)

Reading old documents – old scripts and foreign language alphabets

Old German gothic handwriting and print are very different from the handwriting that you are familiar in today's writing. Many letters and compound consonants were formed very differently. Notice that in the illustration below the letters f, h, j, s and t are very similar and differ only by the location of the loop or no loop. Also the letters h, s and t are formed very differently from what we see today. The second illustration below shows examples of compound consonants that are not used in today's writings but must be recognized in the older documents you will be reviewing in your genealogy research. The interpretation of these letters led to many mistakes in the indexing of names and understanding German Script will help you interpret the correct spelling on the town names that you find in your research.

Concerns in recognizing German Script letters
Notice how the letter "h" in German script looks similar to an "f".

Roman Type	German Script			
f, h, j, s, t	*f*	*f*	*j*	*t*	*t*
a, u, v	*u*	*ü*	*v*		
g, p, y, z	*g*	*p*	*y*	*z*	
e, n	*e*	*n*			

German Script Compound Consonants
Notice how the consonant combinations are very difficult to recognize.

Roman Type

German Script

Roman Type	German Script
ch	*(script)*
sch	*(script)*
ck	*(script)*
ss	*(script)*
ß (SZ, SS)	*(script)*
st	*(script)*
tz	*(script)*
ph	*(script)*

Appendix B at the end of this book is a comparison of Roman Type and Old German Gothic Script and you can obtain a German Gothic Handwriting Guide from Family History Center Wiki at:

https://wiki.familysearch.org/en/images/c/ca/German_Gothic_Handwriting_Guide.pdf

Another factor in your interpretation of the records is the makeup of the alphabets that were used in the documents you will be reviewing. The book "The Paper Trail" by Jonathan D. Shea includes charts of these alphabets and you will need to reference these charts to interpret the documents accurately. See the next section on translating documents for a detail description of Mr. Shea's book.

Translation Books
The language used for the records that you find will be in Latin or the language of the governing country. As you browse the images you should have a list of key words such as dates and relationships to help you select the images that may pertain to your ancestors. You will be able to assemble your list from various genealogy books that have glossary of these terms. Modern translation dictionaries will not normally include the terms that you find in these older documents because languages have changed over time and many terms have fallen out of use and replaced with more modern terms.

Below is a portion of my "Polish Cheat Sheet". I have this sheet of genealogy terms near me when I am browsing through records. This helps me recognize the records that pertain to my ancestors. Note that my cheat sheet has three basic columns – numbers, months and family relationships. These columns are used to recognize the date and the relationships of the people listed on the records. After I have found possible records, I use older dictionaries and books that have larger lists of terms to translate the records further.

My Polish "Cheat Sheet"

English	Polish		English	Polish		English	Polish
1	jeden, pewien		Jan	Styczen		Son	syn
2	dwa		Feb	Luty		Son-in-law	Ziec
3	trzy		March	Marzec		grandson	wnuk
4	cztery		April	Kwiecien		daughter	corka
5	piec		May	Maj		granddaughter	wnuczka
6	szesc		June	Czerwiec		mother	matka
7	siedem		July	Lipiec		grandmother	babka
8	osm		Aug	Sierien		father	rozic, ojciec
9	dziewiec		Sept	Wrzesien		grandfather	dziad, dziadek
10	dziesiec.		Oct	Pazdziernik		great	pra-
11	jedenascie		Nov	Listopad		widow	wdow
12	dwanascie		Dec	Grudzien		wife	zona, matzonka
13	trzynascie					widower	wdowiec
14	czternascie					husband	matzonek, maz, gospodarowac oszczedinc
15	fietnascie					wife of	-cianka

One book that is useful for translation help is *Follow the Paper Trail* by Jonathan D. Shea and William F. Hoffman. It is a guide to translating vital records in 13 languages: Czech, French, German, Hungarian, Italian, Latin, Lithuanian, Polish, Portuguese, Romanian, Russian, Spanish and Swedish. Each section shows the alphabet of the language, sample vital records and their translation. It also includes lists of words commonly encountered in each of the languages.

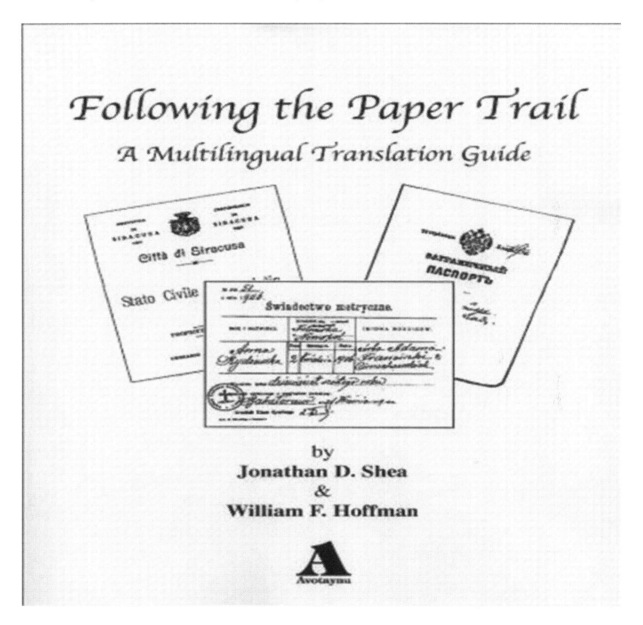

Other Translation Books

Books that I have used to aid in the translation of my Polish records have been:

- *Going Home: A Guide to Polish American Family History Research* by Jonathan Shea
  Jonathan Shea's new guide is an indispensable reference book for anyone doing Polish genealogy research. Going Home covers every possible topic one would need to know about including a history of Poland and Polonia; genealogical resources and records in the U.S.; information about gazetteers and maps; vital records in Poland; vocabulary lists for Polish, Latin, Russian and German; and a discourse on Polish surnames. Three appendices provide information on Polish parishes in the U.S., genealogy web sites, and addresses for archives in Poland, Belarus, Germany, Lithuania, and Ukraine.

- ***In Their Words – Polish*** by Jonathan D. Shea and William F. Hoffman
  Acclaimed translation guides written with the Polish genealogist in mind. This guide analyzes in detail dozens of documents in Polish that your research is likely to encounter – and not just birth, marriage and death records but also passports, obituaries, population registers, military service records, and so on. *It also* gives information on the Polish alphabet, spelling, pronunciation, and standard handwriting; lists thousands of the terms most often encountered in documents; provides information on how to locate records in America and Europe; offers a series of maps illustrating the history of Poland; and includes a whole chapter on using gazetteers to locate your ancestral villages and thus determine which archives are likely to have documents relating to your family, along with contact information for those archives and help writing letters to them.

- ***In Their Words – Russian*** by Jonathan D. Shea and William F. Hoffman
  This guide reviews the same documents and follows the same format as "In Their Words – Polish" but with the Russian language's alphabet, spelling, pronunciation, and standard handwriting and lists thousands of the Russian terms most often encountered in documents.

- ***A Translation Guide to 19th Century Polish-Language Civil-Registration Documents*** by Judith R. Frazin (this book is excellent to translate the polish records that are in the narrative format) This user-friendly and practical resource for anyone with roots in Poland makes suggestions on how to locate ancestral towns on a modern map, determine if old vital records exist, and learn how to acquire, decipher and translate the records. The 472 page book includes a step-by-step guide on how to divide each document into a series of "mini-documents"; seven sample documents with important words and the information which follows these words highlighted; and fifteen topical vocabulary lists, such as Age, Family and Occupations, which include words that occur in 19th century documents.

Other Sources of Genealogy Word Lists

The "wiki" pages at Familysearch.org also have word lists that list many genealogical terms found on various vital records in different in English and the native language for the records. Use the search function to find each list by country or language.

Summary of finding and translating records

- Check familysearch.org online databases to start search
- Next check the databases at Ancestry.com
- If not in online databases at familysearch.org or ancstry.com check FHC catalog to order films
- Check Familysearch.org Wiki pages to find other online databases
- Learn to read German Script and other alphabets
- Use books with glossary of terms to help & older dictionaries to translate records
- Have list of genealogical terms found on vital records (cheat sheet) available when browsing records to help find records of interest.

Desperate Measures for Brickwalls

Use of Genealogy Message Boards

There are many great opportunities to share and exchange information on the internet. One method to do this is through message boards. Message boards can be great tools for genealogists who are trying to connect with others who have similar interests. When many people participate in these boards, the amount of information that can be shared is tremendous. Message boards are also very convenient and researchers are able to search previous posts to the boards and ask questions to other interested readers around the world 24 hours a day, 7 days a week, 365 days a year.

Genforum.com

Genforum is one of the popular message boards. It requires the researcher to select one of their forums – a surname, country, US state or US county. Below is a screen print of Genforum's home page that shows multiple selections available to the researcher. On the left you can select a letter to go to a surname forum or a country or a US state. You can also type the name of a forum in the text box in the upper right corner and go to a specific forum that you already know the title.

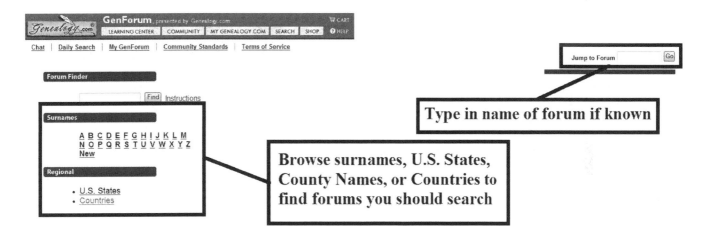

Search Genforum for information

Once you have selected a forum, you can type a key word in the "Search this Forum" text box to narrow the number of posts to review. Next review the headings to select the posts to open and read.

If you need to post a question to this forum, click "Post New Message". You will need to be a registered user and sign in to post this new message or answer a previous post.

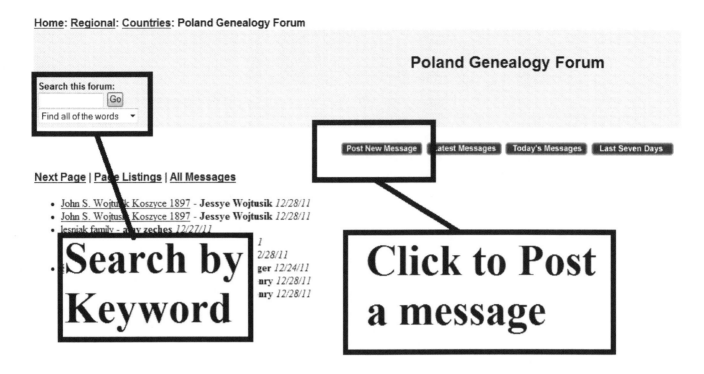

Home: Regional: Countries: Poland Genealogy Forum

Poland Genealogy Forum

Search this forum:
[ ] [Go]
Find all of the words ▼

Post New Message | Latest Messages | Today's Messages | Last Seven Days

Next Page | Page Listings | All Messages

- John S. Wojtusik Koszyce 1897 - **Jessye Wojtusik** *12/28/11*
- John S. Wojtusik Koszyce 1897 - **Jessye Wojtusik** *12/28/11*
- lesniak family - **amy zeches** *12/27/11*

Search by Keyword

Click to Post a message

Below is an earlier post that has been opened and below the message is numerous posts of the thread of replies.

Home: Regional: Countries: Hungary Genealogy Forum

Post Followup | Return to Message Listings | Print Message

Re: Szerna name

Posted by: Stephen Szabados (ID *****9169)

In Reply to: Re: Szerna name by JosephLaszloKupan

I am 100 per cent sure it is Pankota in Arad county (now Romania).

1. Before he died, my grandfather told me he was from Transylvania and it was transferred from Hngary to Romania after World War I.

2. His and his father's naturalization documents also listed that they were from Pankota, Arad County Hungary.

3. I have also tracked over 100 families that immigrated from Arad county to Bloomington, Illinois USA about the same time as my ancestors. All worked at

Notify Administrator about this message?

Followups:

- Re: Szerna name **JosephLaszloKupan** *4/02/09*
  - Re: Szerna name **Stephen Szabados** *4/02/09*
    - Re: Szerna name **JosephLaszloKupan** *4/02/09*
      - Re: Szerna name **Stephen Szabados** *4/02/09*

Post Followup | Return to Message Listings | Print Message

Below is the text of a reply to one of my posts on Genforum that was finally answered after about nine months of waiting.

Heading: *Chmielewski, Zaluski, Zuchowski, Dmochowski, Dmochy, Czyzew, Andrzejewo*
Date: *Sunday, August 17, 2008 4:59 PM*

From: *"xxxxxxx xxxxxxxxx" <xxxxxxx@yahoo.co.uk>*

View contact details
To: xxxxxxxxxxxx@sbcglobal.net

Hi:-) I accidently found your post :

My grandparents were born in Andrzejewo and Dmochy Kudly near Czyzew and south of Lomza.
I would like to exchange information with anyone that has ancestors from this area and have the
surnames of Chmielewski, Zuchowski, Zaluski and Dmochowski.

My both parents are from Dmochy My dad was born in Dmochy Wochy (Zawistowski) and my mum in
Dmochy Kudly(Malinowska but her mother's maiden name Dmochowska) .I am living in UK but my
parents are living in Poland in Czyzew and I got my Godfather living in Dmochy so I can ask them some
questions if you want

Kindly Regards
Pawel

After numerous exchanges of emails and information it was determined that I was probably related to Pawel's mother. Also Pawel's mother visited the village and borrowed a number of pictures from descendants of my grandfather's brother and below is a picture of my great-grandfather Leopold Zuchowski that Pawel sent to me. This is a great treasure for a little effort.

Leopold Zuchowski – my Great-grandfather

Rootsweb.com

Rootsweb is another website that offers a popular message board. Below is a screen print of the Rootsweb homepage with the Message Board selection option highlighted. The next page shown below is the "Message Board" page and the text box that you will use to search all of the Rootsweb messages. You can also select specific boards to search.

Rootsweb.com Home Page

Rootsweb Message Board

Below is a Sample of results for a search for the surname Dmochowski which is highlighted automatically by Rootsweb software.

Re: Maiden Name of Helen Pietruszka
Surnames > Pietruszka

Do you know if Rose Dmochowski was married to Alexander?

Re: Maiden Name of Helen Pietruszka
Surnames > Pietruszka

Yes, Rose's husband was Alex Dmochowski, they lived in Camden, NJ. Annie her sister, my grandmother married Alexander (

Re: Maiden Name of Helen Pietruszka
Surnames > Pietruszka

My grandfather was the cousin of Alex Dmochowski and I think he and my grandmother met in Camden when my grandfathe

Guidelines and tips to follow when using Message Boards:
1. Only post information on a message board that you are comfortable with being made public. Read your post carefully before you click the send or post button.
2. Read the user agreement for the message board and follow their guideline carefully.
3. Include as much information as possible that pertains to your question or response to avoid confusion. More details should produce responses that are more appropriate to the question.
4. Please type using correct spelling and correct grammar – again to avoid confusion.
5. Be considerate and polite to others at all times.

Use Online Family Trees for Clues

Many websites allow researchers to post the family trees online. Although researchers may use offline lineage software to build their family trees, they may also use online trees. Many of these trees were the researchers initial attempt to save the results of their research but researchers have also found the online trees is an excellent tool to make contact with other people searching for the same ancestors and exchange information. Please remember that this information may be very exciting to find but you must do the work and verify its accuracy.
1. The value of searching online family trees would be to provide clues on where to look for the next level in your family tree.
2. The value of maintaining your family tree online is to make contacts with researchers to exchange information.

Below is a sample of the Ancestry.com page that allows a subscriber to search Ancestry's database of family trees. Most other family tree websites offer similar options.

Below is the Ancestry.com page for my grandfather's information. If you have an online family tree only for an online presence, you can post as much or as few details as you desire. It is recommended that you post some details to attract responses from other researchers. The amount of details that I posted for my grandfather may be more extensive than is needed to attract a researcher but I added more information to exchange information with close relatives that I had already contacted and allowed them to visit the family tree without being a subscriber.

Contact from someone seeing one of my family trees on Ancestry.com

Below is an email that I received from a woman in Germany who turned out to be my daughter-in-law's third cousin and had just started her research. I shared my US research with her and she sent me a small list of German ancestors plus a picture of the house that my daughter-in-law's ancestor sold to bring his family to America. The picture of the house follows the email.

Here is the Email from Katrina in Germany about my daughter-in-law's family tree:

Itch have Hire Profile auf Ancestry - refunded, in deem waiter Informational angefordert werden
Sunday, July 13, 2008 12:45 PM

From: Katrin
To: "steve_szabados" <antiquebookworm@sbcglobal.net>

Hi, I`m from Germany, doing research in my ancestry...I`m a grandchild of a born "Volk" from Wahles, Thuringia. Are you related to John and Terry XXXXXX???

Greets from Germany! Kathrin

House that ancestor of daughter-in-law sold to immigrate to Illinois (picture supplied by Katrin)

Concerns when posting your family tree on the internet:
- Upload your tree to Ancestry.com – this may get you questions from other people who are researching the same people as you are.
- Be careful to avoid posting information that is private or that you do not want known outside of the family – such as birth, Social Security Number, etc
- Be as accurate as possible. Try to post only confirmed facts to our online tree.

Summary of Points to Help you Find Grandma
- Use multiple documents to find place names related to your ancestors that can be used to find clusters of towns on a map. This is needed because many town names have multiple locations and looking for multiple town names that should be in the nearby area will allow the accurate locating of your ancestor's birthplace.
- Go back to school – learn the history of border changes in the areas that your ancestors left.

- Know the history of border changes in the country and various counties and areas. This will help you search the correct map.
- Be prepared to translate the documents that you find. Use language word lists of genealogical terms.
- Be patient – it may take time to find the correct map, the documents that list the place names and receive the FHC films
- Be thorough – collect all of the possible documents and exhausted your search for information before moving on to the next step.
- Revisit sources as you obtain more facts. Also online databases add new content regularly.

Appendix A – Useful Websites and books

General

- Cindi's list - http://www.cyndislist.com/
- Ancestry.com
- Ellisisland.org
- NARA - http://www.archives.gov/
- Family History Centers - http://www.familysearch.org
- Illinois Archives Databases - http://www.cyberdriveillinois.com/departments/archives/databases.html
- Illinois State Genealogical Society - http://www.rootsweb.ancestry.com/~ilsgs/
- Footnote - http://www.footnote.com/
- Rootweb.com
- Genforum.com
- Bureau of Land Management - http://www.glorecords.blm.gov/
- Sanborn maps - http://www.loc.gov/rr/geogmap/sanborn/
- Genealogy Trails History Group - http://genealogytrails.com/
- Language translation - http://mylanguageexchange.com/
- Austrian Maps - http://lazarus.elte.hu/hun/digkonyv/topo/3felmeres.htm
- Interviewing tips - http://genealogy.about.com/cs/oralhistory/a/interview.htm
- Book - Give Your Family a Gift That Money Can't Buy: Record & Preserve Your Family's History by Jeffrey Bockman
- Book - First steps in genealogy : a beginner's guide to researching your family history by Desmond Walls Allen

Chicago & Cook County

- Newberry Library- http://www.newberry.org/
- Chicago Genealogy - http://www.chicagogenealogy.com/
- Cook County Clerk's Genealogy records - http://www.cookcountygenealogy.com
- Cook County Naturalization records - http://www.cookcountyclerkofcourt.org/NR/about.aspx
- Chicago Parish locator - http://www.rootsweb.ancestry.com/~itappcnc/cathsearch.htm
- Cook county Cemeteries - http://www.rootsweb.ancestry.com/~itappcnc/pipcncookcem.htm

Czech

- Czech & Slovak American Genealogy Society of Illinois - http://www.csagsi.org/
- Family Search Wiki for the Czech Republic - https://wiki.familysearch.org/en/Czech_Republic
- Czech State Regional Digital Archives
    - Trebon - http://digi.ceskearchivy.cz/index_main.php?lang=en
    - **Prague - http://www.ahmp.cz**
    - **Plzeň** - http://www.soaplzen.cz/
    - **Litoměřice** - http://www.soalitomerice.cz
    - **Zámrsk** - http://www.vychodoceskearchivy.cz
    - **Brno -** http://www.mza.cz
    - **Opava** - http://www.archives.cz
- Czech Genealogy - http://www.iarelative.com/czech/
- FEEFHS (The Federation of East European Family History Societies) - http://www.feefhs.org/
- Index of Chicago Czech obituaries - **The Denni Hlasatel obituary index, 1971-1995 by Joe Novak**
- Obtain copies of Chicago Czech obituaries - www.mollx.com (Springfield, Illinois researcher

Employment Records
- Chicago and Northwestern Historical Society – employment records
- South Suburban Genealogy Society – employees records for Pullman Car works (manufacturing)
- Railroad Retirement Board – all railroad employees
- IRAD Regional Archive – Chicago Civil Service Promotional Registers 1895 to 1950
- Newberry Library – Pullman Car service employees (porters, etc)
- Newberry Library – Chicago Board of Education Directory (1895, 1896, 1900-1909, 1928 and 1929 and Chicago Board of Education Annual Report (1859–1870, 1872-1915 and 1918)
- Harold Washington Library Reference Center - Chicago Board of Education Directory (1897-1954) and Chicago Board of Education Annual Report (1867 – 1925)

England & Scotland
- UK and Scottish online database - Find My Past – www.findmypast.co.uk
- Scotland's People – www.scotlandspeople.gov.uk
- Gens Reunited - http://www.genesreunited.co.uk/
- Lists of UK and Scottishgenealogy websites – www.genuki.org.uk
- National Archives of Scotland – www.nas.gov.uk
- The National Archives of UK – www.nationalarchives.gov.uk
- National Library of Scotland – www.nls.uk

German
- German Genealogy Group - http://www.germangenealogygroup.com/
- German Genealogy Internet Portal - http://www.genealogienetz.de/genealogy.html
- Cindi's List German links - http://www.cyndislist.com/germany.htm
- German Roots - http://www.germanroots.com/
- German Gazetteer – Meyer Ort – (find at Familysearch.org on German wiki)
- Kartenmeister (www.kartenmeister.com) – excellent website for finding modern names of towns of the Oder and Neisse Rivers
- ShtetlSeeker Town Searchhttp://www.jewishgen.org/communities/loctown.asp
- Chicago Area Lutheran churches - http://www.elca.org/Who-We-Are/History/ELCA-Archives.aspx

Hungarian
- Hungarian Schwabian Village search - http://www.dvhh.org/web1/villageindex.php
- Donauschwaben in the Banat - http://www.genealogienetz.de/reg/ESE/dsbanat.html
- History of German Settlements in Southern Hungary - http://www.genealogienetz.de/reg/ESE/dshist.txt
- 1882 gazetteer of Hungary - http://www.bogardi.com/gen/g104.shtml
- The History of the Danube Swabians by Hans Kopp - http://www.donauschwaben-usa.org/history.htm

Irish
- Find My Past Ireland - http://www.findmypast.ie
- Irish Genealogy - http://www.irishgenealogy.ie/
- Chicago Jewish Archives - http://www.spertus.edu/
- Chicago Jewish Historical Society - http://www.chicagojewishhistory.org/
- Jewish Genealogical Society of Illinois (JGSI)   - http://www.jewishgen.org/jgsi/
- Irish Ancestors - http://www.irishancestors.net/
- The Irish Genealogical Society (IGSI) - http://www.irishgenealogical.org/
- Ireland genealogy projects - http://irelandgenealogyprojects.rootsweb.ancestry.com/

Jewish

- JewishGen - The Home of Jewish Genealogy - http://www.jewishgen.org/
- Chicago Jewish Archives - http://www.spertus.edu/
- Chicago Jewish Historical Society - http://www.chicagojewishhistory.org/
- Jewish Genealogical Society of Illinois (JGSI)   - http://www.jewishgen.org/jgsi/
- ShtetlSeeker Town Search (www.jewishgen.org/communities/loctown.asp)

Polish

- Family Search Polish Portal - https://wiki.familysearch.org/en/Poland
- Polish Genealogy Society of America - http://pgsa.org/
- Polish Translation - http://www.poltran.com
- Polish satellite maps - http://www.zumi.pl/
- Posen Genealogy - http://www.posen-l.com/
- Posen Marriage Project - http://bindweed.man.poznan.pl/posen/search.php
- Polish Roots - http://www.polishroots.org/
- the internet Polish Genealogical Source (iPGS) - http://www.ipgs.us/
- Polish & German names for villages in Poland - http://prussianpoland.com/germanpolishnamespoland.html
- Polish-German place names - http://www.atsnotes.com/other/gerpol.html
- Old Maps of Germany - http://www.maxpages.com/poland/Maps_and_Towns_Germany
- Polish Germany towns - http://www.kartenmeister.com/preview/databaseuwe.asp
- **Book- Following the paper trail : a multilingual translation guide by Jonathan D. Shea & William F. Hoffman**
- **Book- In their words : a genealogist's translation guide to Polish, German, Latin, and Russian documents by Jonathan D. Shea and William F. Hoffman**
- **Book-** Going Home – A Guide to Polish American Family Research by **Jonathan D. Shea**
- **Book-** A translation guide to 19th-century Polish-language civil-registration documents : including birth, marriage and death records by Judith R. Frazin
- **Book- First names of the Polish commonwealth : origins & meanings / by William F. Hoffman and George Wiesław Helon**
- **Book- Polish surnames : origins and meanings / William F. Hoffman**

Swedish

- Swedish Online records – http://www.Ancestry.com (World Edition or Library Edition)- Swedish church records 1500 to 1937 (originally Genline)

Italian

- Italian affiliate for Ancestry.com - http://www.ancestry.it/ (note in Italian)
- Northwest suburban Italian chapter of Pointers in Person - http://www.rootsweb.ancestry.com/~itappcnc/index.htm
- Italian Town database by Dan Niemiec - http://www.rootsweb.ancestry.com/~itappcnc/pipcntown.htm

Old German Type and Handwriting

Roman Type	German Type	German Script		Roman Type	German Type	German Script
Aa	𝔄a			Vv	𝔙v	
Bb	𝔅b			Ww	𝔚w	
Cc	ℭc			Xx	𝔛x	
Dd	𝔇d			Yy	𝔜y	
Ee	𝔈e			Zz	ℨ	
Ff	𝔉f					
Gg	𝔊g			**Modified Vowels (Umlaute)**		
Hh	ℌh					
Ii	ℑi			Ää	𝔄ä	
Jj	𝔍j			Öö	𝔒ö	
Kk	𝔎f			Üü	𝔘ü	
Ll	𝔏l					
Mm	𝔐m			**Compound Consonants**		
Nn	𝔑n					
Oo	𝔒o			ch	𝔠𝔥	
Pp	𝔓p			sch	𝔰𝔠𝔥	
Qq	𝔔q			ck	𝔠𝔨	
Rr	𝔕r			ss	𝔰𝔰	
Ss	𝔖𝔰			ß (SZ, SS)	ß (ß 𝔰𝔰)	
Tt	𝔗t			st	𝔰𝔱	
Uu	𝔘u			tz	𝔱𝔷	
				ph	𝔭𝔥	

Appendix C - other languages

Polish Alphabet

- In the Polish alphabet there are 32 letters, 9 vowels and 23 consonants
  - *a, ą, b, c, ć, d, e, ę, f, g, h, i, j, k, l, ł, m, n, ń, o, ó, p, r, s, ś, t, u, w, y, z, ź, ż*
  - *Diacriticals for the Polish language such as ogonek (˛), kreska (´)and kropka (·)*
    - *Letters q, v, x are not normally used in Polish*

Hungarian Alphabet

A	Á	B	C	Cs	D	Dz	Dzs	E	É	F	G	Gy	H	I	Í	J	K	L	Ly	M	N
Ny	O	Ó	Ō	Ő	P	(Q)	R	S	Sz	T	Ty	U	Ú	Ü	Ũ	V	(W)	(X)	(Y)	Z	Zs

Czech Alphabet

A, Á, B, C, Č, D, Ď, E, É, Ě, F, G, H, Ch, I, Í, J, K, L, M, N, Ň, O, Ó, P, Q, R, Ř, S, Š, T, Ť, U, Ú, Ů, V, W, X, Y, Ý, Z, Ž

ABOUT THE AUTHOR

Steve Szabados is a native of Bloomington, Illinois and is a retired project manager. He received a Bachelor of Science Degree from the University of Illinois in Champaign-Urbana, Illinois and a Masters in Business Administration from Northern Illinois University in DeKalb, Illinois. He has been researching his ancestors for about ten years and has traced ancestors back to 1600s New England and 1730's in Poland, Germany, Bohemia and Slovenia. He has given numerous presentations to genealogical groups and libraries in Illinois, Indiana and Wisconsin. His goal is to share his passion for Family History. He is a member of the Polish Genealogical Society of America, Northwest Suburban Genealogy Society, Illinois State Genealogical Society and he is also a genealogy volunteer at the Arlington Heights Illinois Library. Steve also is the genealogy columnist for the Polish American Journal and manages his genealogy blog.

12235573R00072

Made in the USA
Charleston, SC
21 April 2012